WILDLIFE & WOODLAND

FACTS & FUN

Experiences of a Wildlife Biologist

To Nan,
Happy Wildlife Watching!
Kent Kammermeyer

Kent Kammermeyer

ISBN: 978-1-61005-204-7

Library of Congress Control Number: 2012940909

Printed in the United States of America by:
BOOKLOGIX˙
Alpharetta, Georgia

♾This paper meets the requirements of ANSI/NISO Z39.48-1992 (Permanence of Paper)

Cover photo credits: Coyote photo by Terry Trammell. All other photos by Kent Kammermeyer. Cover bear sketch by Edith K. Vassar.

WHAT THEY SAY ABOUT WILDLIFE AND WOODLAND FACTS AND FUN

"At last, a book about wildlife that is factual, informative and a lot of fun to read, a rare combination with books of this type. *Wildlife & Woodland Facts & Fun* is cleverly written by one who has been there daily for several decades, Kent Kammermeyer, a wildlife biologist in Georgia. Kent's stories are filled with useful wildlife information on wild critters plus lots of first person adventures he experienced while working with wildlife. Entertaining, yet educational, reading that will keep you coming back for more, a book you will want in your library. Kent has hit a "home run" with this book."

J. Wayne Fears, Outdoorsman/Author/Editor 3-2-12

"This book is a compilation of a lifetime of experiences and accumulated knowledge by a professional wildlifer. It addresses the problems and gratifications of human interactions with animals. It is unique! It will be useful to all people who are interested in animals whether they live in a big city, the suburbs, exurbs or country."

R. Larry Marchinton, Professor Emeritus, Warnell School of Forest Resources, University of Georgia 3-5-12

"Kent Kammermeyer's *Wildlife & Woodland Facts & Fun* presents a first hand, and often humorous, account of personal wildlife and natural world experiences. For the casual outdoor enthusiast to the dedicated hunter and wildlife manager, it's entertaining and educational, a fine addition to any outdoor book collection."

"Just finished reading the book you sent me. It's both informative and entertaining. It's obviously one of those books that could not have been written without the education and knowledge combined with many years of "in the field" experiences. A good read for anyone from homeowners to hunters. Great job!"

"Kent Kammermeyer is as much at home at his keyboard sharing his wealth of knowledge from a lifetime of scientific investigation and outdoor adventures, as he is sitting in his blind waiting for that twelve-point buck to come along. His latest book, *Wildlife & Woodland Facts & Fun*, is eclectic in scope, engagingly written, and merges lots of "how to" with personal comments and anecdotes. It belongs on the bookshelf of every outdoor enthusiast."

DEDICATION

Wildlife & Woodland Facts & Fun is dedicated to the important women in my life: my mom Vanda D., wife Freda, sisters Edee, Kate, Sue, Lynn and daughter Vanda M. My mom passed away in May 1975 at the relatively young age of 60, just before my graduation from The University of Georgia. No doubt she succumbed from the stresses of raising five kids the right way, virtually on her own without much help from our dad. She encouraged me in my chosen field of study, even though it took me over 1,000 miles from home. Not only that, she paid for some of it, as much as she could afford from working at her modest job of lab technician.

Everyone else listed above was also very supportive and tolerant of my profession and associated hobbies despite the fact that it often took me away from them for short and long periods of time. I live over 1,000 miles away from all my sisters and am frequently away from my wife and daughter on weekends, consulting jobs and professional meetings. Thank you all!

From left to right my wife Freda, my sisters
Sue and Edee, and my daughter Vanda

ACKNOWLEDGEMENTS

More than a few good people influenced my journey into wildlife and woodlands. I hope these pages capture most of them but I am sure some will be inadvertently left out. I apologize in advance to these people who were important in guiding my life and career but may have been unintentionally omitted from this book.

I have dedicated *Wildlife & Woodland Facts & Fun* to the important women in my life: my mom, wife, sisters and daughter. See **Dedication** page for more details.

My friend **Charlie Nichols** in Winsted, CT first introduced me to hunting small game and experiencing the woods and all other wildlife at the same time. Later **Rich Kemp** also became a good hunting buddy in the same neck of the woods.

The Boss, **Mr. Jim Zucco**, owner of the Old Riverton Inn, took me under his wing when I was a junior in high school in 1966 and taught me the ropes of hunting big game on his north woods hunting club in NH. His conservation ethic and high regard for healthy wild red meat lives on in me. Those early years are burned in my memory (see Chapter 24) and served to widen the path to my career of wildlife management especially deer management and biology.

From the very beginning, both before and after the passing of The Boss, **Paul Svetz** was a long time hunting buddy and good friend since 1966. With The Boss gone in 2001, Paul took over his club membership and made certain that all of the long standing hunting guests (including me) were invited often again under his watch. He was and still is an extremely accommodating and generous friend.

Dr. Robert McDowell, my major professor at UConn inspired me with his lectures and encouraged me to choose UGA for a MS degree program in Wildlife Biology based on its impressive reputation in wildlife research. This turned out to be some of the best advice in my life.

I enrolled in UGA Forestry School in 1972 and quickly encountered four of the most renowned and inspiring wildlife professors in the USA: **Dr. Jim Jenkins, Dr. Syd Johnson, Dr. Ernie Provost and Dr. Larry Marchinton.** Larry was soon to be my major professor because of his experience and expertise in deer research and deer management. He pushed me pretty hard on my deer thesis and it worked. His thesis pressure on all of his students was affectionately known among us as the "suffering index!" I really appreciate Larry writing the Foreword for this book.

I had highly educational coursework and projects under all four of the above professors. They were unique in that all of them had extensive wildlife field work before becoming UGA professors unlike today's professors who may not spend a day in the field before spending their entire careers in academia. If there were such a thing as the Wildlife Hall of Fame, all four of these professors would be in it.

Several UGA fellow students quickly became my friends despite the fact that I was born and raised a "Yankee" for sure. These included but were not limited to **Neal Eichholz, Vic Vansant, Carroll Allen, Joe Hamilton, James Poplin, Allen Smith, Steve Evans, Ken Grahl, Terry Kile, Tom Atkeson, Larry Landers, Scott Osborne, Phil Hale, Charlie Ford, Reggie Thackston** and others.

More recently, I want to thank my good friends and hunting buddies **Ken Burnette, Tommy Hunter** and **Dr. Tommy Jenkins**. I learned a lot from these guys and I hope they learned something from me. Tommy Hunter is my business partner in **Advanced Wildlife Services, LLC**.

I also learned a lot from **Lindsay Thomas** editor of *Quality Whitetails* magazine and **Dr. Karl Miller**, UGA wildlife professor. Both were co-editors and contributing authors of our *Quality Food Plots* book. I want to thank these fine professionals for all they did for the book and me.

Thanks to **Vanda Kammermeyer, Betty Marchinton** and **Bobbie Lancaster** for editing parts of this book and making valuable suggestions on format, consistency and content.

This book was inspired by my friend **Milt Smith** author of *Wildlife Whimsy*, published in 2009. I helped him with his book and in the process was able to pattern my book after his shortly afterwards. He made me think "Why can't I do this?" The answer is I can.

Finally, I want to thank my friend and co-author of our second book, **Reggie Thackston**, who authored most of the turkey management and some of the deer management content in *Deer & Turkey Management Beyond Food Plots*. Reggie stuck his neck out for the book on blind faith not just by contributing manuscripts but also paying for a good part of the publishing and printing costs. He is my partner through **Kent Kammermeyer Consulting, LLC**.

TABLE OF CONTENTS

FOREWORD

Human populations are expanding into the country as one time wild lands are becoming rural and areas once rural are now exurban. Suburbs are melding into the urban population as more and more people live in cities. Cities are spreading then coalescing to become continuous but most wildlife seems to be adapting to what can accurately be called a human octopus. Once wild lands and even wilderness areas are now too civilized for big wide ranging predatory species such as wolves and Eastern cougars. On the other hand, deer, coyotes, raccoons, birds and many other species have learned to exist in suburbs and even cities. Black bear and wild hog populations have exploded in the Eastern United States over the past 20 years. Consequently, people-wildlife contacts, good or bad, have been rapidly increasing. Folks have mixed opinions or notions about all of these animals and often lack the basic information needed to coexist with them.

Many people in cities, suburbs and country keep pets. Companion animals occupy greater roles in human life and they are commonly thought of as family members. Pet and working animals are intermingling more with wild animal populations even in cities. I'm sure this is why there are three chapters in this book dealing with domestic pets mixed in with lots of wildlife and woodland chapters. In addition, human interactions with animals, both wild and domestic, are not diminishing, but the ways we interact with animals are changing, and creating puzzling questions and dilemmas.

The author of this book, Kent Kammermeyer was a graduate student working with me nearly 38 years ago. Since then, he has been a close friend and for a number of years, a hunting buddy. As a student, he learned from me but in his years as a wildlife researcher, manager and biologist I have learned from him. Kent has authored several books over the years. Recently, he requested that I read this book and write a foreword. The subject matter is different from those he has written before. Although I taught university courses in wildlife biology for thirty years, there were many new and interesting things to me in every chapter.

This book is a compilation of a lifetime of experiences and accumulated knowledge by a professional wildlifer. It addresses the problems and gratifications of human interactions with animals. It is unique! It will be useful to all people who are interested in animals whether they live in a big city, the suburbs, exurbs or country. Even university trained wildlife specialists can benefit from reading it. In fact, anyone who considers themselves wildlife watchers or deals with any kind of vertebrate animal problem, has pets, or views, studies, hunts or otherwise interacts with wild or companion animals will find it a valuable reference and an interesting read.

R. Larry Marchinton, Professor Emeritus, Warnell School of Forest Resources, University of Georgia

PREFACE

I am a Certified Wildlife Biologist (since 1979) who grew up in rural Connecticut in the 1950's and 1960's and worked several summers on a dairy farm in New Hampshire. I always had a fascination for and appreciation of animals and wildlife, and thanks to my friends, turned this into lifelong hobbies of fishing and hunting. After graduating from the University of Connecticut and the University of Georgia with majors in wildlife management and wildlife biology, I spent a 30 year career with Georgia Department of Natural Resources, Wildlife Resources Division doing deer management and deer research. In addition, I spent time answering complaints and providing information on wildlife and wildlife-related topics to the general public. In my last five to 10 years, I logged about 300 contacts per year. The information and experiences I included in this book are universal to the Appalachian Mountains, the eastern half of the United States and beyond.

The book is a collection of my best columns published in *The Gainesville Times* newspaper over a 10-year period as well as my articles which appeared in *Quality Whitetails* magazine and *Georgia Outdoor News* magazine. They are revised, updated, expanded and enhanced to appeal more to a general audience where interest in wildlife remains acute but the information base is very scattered and sketchy. There is also lots of misinformation and lack of communication among wildlife scientists and lay persons thereby fueling a basic misunderstanding and fear about woodlands, wildlife and their identification, movements and habits. Moreover, mixed with the facts are often amusing true stories as they unfolded along the way either over the phone or in the field.

This book is for anyone even remotely interested in wildlife and the outdoors including homeowners, hikers, hunters, bird watchers, gardeners, photographers, bikers, pet owners, farmers, horse riders and every other outdoor enthusiast and wildlife watcher. Readers will surely learn a lot of wildlife-related facts that are very interesting. The book is easy reading, factual, informative, fun and entertaining!

Not just about furred and feathered wildlife, the book also includes true woodland stories from researched facts and the author's personal experiences about dogs, cats, Lyme disease, and a truly beloved mentor named "The Boss" who passed away peacefully in his sleep in February 2001. See chapters 11, 13, 23 and 24.

I hope you enjoy the book as well as my talented sister Edee's sketches! Thanks for your interest! Visit my website at www.deerconsulting.com

Kent Kammermeyer

Clermont, Georgia

April, 2012

BLACK BEARS
GETTING IN TROUBLE

Bears are almost always in the news in May, June and July. This is true all over the eastern half of the country! Our bears live in the North Georgia mountains but are frequent visitors in counties just south of the mountains all the way to Atlanta. These vagabonds are almost always yearlings weighing about 100 pounds and traveling mostly in the late spring and early summer. Bears crossing through regions with high human activity are frequently road-killed. Have you ever tried crossing an interstate highway or a four-lane state highway near a major metro area? It is not easy for a human or a bear, especially after dark! Most of the time, vehicles that hit bears are totaled. Drivers and passengers are sometimes seriously injured or killed. Georgia wildlife officials don't track the number of bear-vehicle collisions, but authorities say three bears were killed in a 10-day span in June 2011 alone as a result of crashes with motorists on North Georgia roads.

They have been seen swimming across coves on some very large lakes all over North Georgia. Yes, black bears are very good swimmers! I can recall at least three incidents of residents or boaters reporting bears swimming on different parts of 35,000-acre Lake Lanier. They funnel to the lake by traveling downstream along two big river systems which converge to form the lake. River systems, with their wooded floodplains, are favorite travel corridors for wandering bears.

Sightings of these bears are common along the Appalachian Trail. A few bears have learned to tear into hikers properly stored food supplies suspended high above the ground between trees by chewing through the rope and dropping food to the ground for dinner. Recently, near the southern end of the trail, six or eight campers yelling and jumping up and down failed to run a bear off of their food.

Yonah Mountain (near Helen, Georgia) recently harbored a sow with a big family of four yearling cubs that were getting into trouble. They entered a house through an unlocked door and made a mess of the kitchen cabinets, extracting all the food they could possibly find! This behavior is rare, but the bad news is this unusual boldness is obviously dangerous for both people and bears. It happens wherever black bears exist near houses and over time lose their fear of people. Georgia DNR's Game Management section trapped two of the bears in one trap, tagged them and moved them to more remote bear habitat about 15 miles to the northwest.

Normally, this is far enough to keep them from finding their way back home, but that was not the case this time. All five bears were seen together again around Yonah not long after the move. Sometimes the stress of the trap, tranquilizer, and ear-tagging, weighing and other manipulations by humans is enough to deter any further nuisance activities by the offending bears. With this bear family, it worked! They have never been reported in a nuisance situation again.

June is the main month for dispersal of yearling bears into suburbs, so wildlife officials worry that increased bear activity may continue at least until blackberries ripen and provide their main summer food supply. Mostly, the suburb damage is done by displaced young male bears pushed out of their normal mountain range by dominant male bears and their own mothers during the June breeding season. They wander through suburbs seeking food in the form of sunflower seeds in bird feeders, hummingbird nectar, barbeque grills, pet food and garbage cans.

Practice your own preventative measures by removing or securing all of these items especially bird feeders and garbage. Take down bird feeders for the summer and move trash cans behind locked doors. Move hummingbird feeders and suspend them on a cable at least 10 feet above the ground. Bolt or lock all outbuildings and doors in the home. See more details in chapter two.

Do not under any circumstances feed bears! It is dangerous for you and a death sentence for the bears which will gradually lose their fear of people. Left alone with no food available, all bears will wander away without incident. These highly populated areas are not bear habitat, and they should not be encouraged to linger. They get there by mistake, pushed away from mama bear because of breeding season, and they will leave on their own if they can find a way out; eventually most do. Large river systems including the Chattahoochee, Chestatee, Etowah and Oconee here in Georgia are their preferred normal travel corridors because of wooded floodplains with less human development and activity.

Occasionally, wildlife biologists are reluctantly forced by the media and police departments to chase suburban bears around with dart guns attempting to catch the animals and relocate them back to the mountains where they came from. This is mostly a futile effort and bad for the bears, sometimes pushing them into traffic. They often end up dead on the highway or wandering aimlessly even farther than before, looking for a way out of their suburban predicament. Trouble also occurs when dogs chase bears up a tree in someone's yard and a crowd gathers around the tree to gawk and snap photos on their cell phones. Sometimes police officers and firemen come, and they do the same thing! Sooner or later (mostly later) someone figures out, "Gee whiz, you know if we move these dogs and people out of here, the bear will come down on his own and run away from here as fast as he can go."

If they are successfully captured by dart gun or culvert trap (a 48- inch, 10-foot long steel culvert with a pedal trigger and heavy guillotine door), they are most often inadvertently transported and dumped in unfamiliar territory in the home range of a dominant male bear who promptly runs them out, and the process starts all over again. Despite wearing ear tags, few transported bears are ever heard from again.

Several years ago, biologist David Carlock and I happened to be together at the main DNR office in Atlanta for some reason that I cannot remember. Trying to beat the traffic, we left to return to our office in Gainesville about 3 p.m. It was not long until we received a radio call about several bear sightings in the city of Marietta near a high school with subdivisions all around it. This is a highly populated area and no place for a bear. We had a dart gun in the truck, were the closest biologists to the area and reluctantly responded. Chasing a bear around on the ground and catching him with a dart gun is incredibly difficult as we both knew from experience. It is like finding a needle in a haystack.

We arrived at the scene in a subdivision where there was a big crowd gathered along with an Atlanta TV reporter who immediately stuck a microphone in our faces. It seemed like only a few seconds before someone shouted "There he goes!" We saw the bear race across a lawn and into a small patch of woods behind a house. We quickly loaded a dart with a tranquilizing drug, instructed the crowd to stay back, and went quietly into the woods. Lo and behold, there he was 30 yards in front of us looking frightened and confused by all the commotion. David took a shot and hit him just right, in the hindquarter. Now came the hard part, when the bear gets a full five or 10 minutes to run anywhere he wants to go until the drug takes effect! We waited the full 10 minutes, enlisted some brave volunteers, and began the search, noting we could see houses in the distance all around the back side of the small wooded patch. Not long after, we heard someone shout "Here he is!" We ran to the spot and saw him lying next to a pool of water in dense woods with part of his nose submerged. We pulled him back and verified that he was still breathing! It was a long hot walk to the truck lugging a 100-pound bear, but we got there and loaded him in the pickup bed as we did not have a culvert trap with us. After a few words with the TV reporter, we pulled out and headed north toward bear country. I can't remember which one of us said it, but one of us said "Can you believe it? How lucky can we get?"

Then we hit a big rush hour traffic jam in a busy northern suburb of Atlanta. While sitting at a red light, we felt the truck begin to rock a little. We looked back and saw the bear sitting up and wobbling back and forth, signs that he was recovering from the drug. Drivers behind us who were witnessing the event started honking their horns. I quickly loaded a syringe, got out and stuck him in the hip. In just a couple of minutes, he slumped over and went back to sleep. We got out of there by the skin of our teeth, thankful that he did not have enough of his faculties to jump out of the back of the truck into all of that traffic! We got to our office, loaded him into a trap and parked him in the shade. The next day we took all of our measurements, pulled a tiny tooth for aging, tagged both ears and pulled him 50 miles north into the mountains, never to hear from him again. What an adventure!

Young black bears on the move seem to have a habit of getting into all sorts of trouble in the spring and summer – raiding bee hives, corn fields, garbage cans, backyard bird feeders, camping areas, or maybe just wandering through the middle of a city on a Saturday night looking for an escape route (that has actually happened several times). Fortunately, however, they are mostly very fearful of humans and dogs and try to avoid them at all costs. Unlike grizzly bears, which do not occur in Georgia or anywhere in the eastern states, black bears are not at all aggressive. They are totally driven by food and finding a territory they can call home.

BEARS IN
YOUR BACKYARD

Have you seen any bears in your neighborhood? If your answer is no, then that's the way it is supposed to be. Wild black bears are shy and secretive, and even high-density bear populations rarely exceed about one per square mile (640 acres).

If your answer is yes, then you already have potential for close encounters of the bear kind. When bears are highly visible, especially during daylight hours, it is a sign bears are losing their natural fear of people, usually because of food handouts, intentional or not. **Please don't feed the bears!** Feeding bears is not healthy for you or the bear!

Nuisance bears have been known to destroy trash cans, bird feeders, corn fields and bee hives. In the past, some extremely bold individuals, emboldened after years of handouts, have entered outbuildings or even houses through screen doors and windows. Obviously, this can be a serious situation with potential for surprise encounters for people and bears.

The best solution to any potential bear problems is prevention. If the bear never gets a human handout, chances are good that both parties will live happily ever after. To ensure your safety and that of the bear, please follow this simple guideline while visiting or living in bear country: never feed bears by accident or purposely! Bears can easily open refrigerators and coolers and climb into pickup truck beds. Don't throw table scraps out in your yard or off the back porch.

If you feed birds, hang bird seed in feeders suspended at least 10- feet high. Consider switching away from sunflower seed. Don't throw seed on the ground or on your deck. Stop bird feeding altogether in spring and summer; birds don't need feed in these seasons when natural food supplies are relatively abundant .

Secure your garbage cans with a latch or lock. Remove your trash at frequent intervals – every day before dusk if possible. Do not leave dog or cat food outside overnight or unattended. Feed your animals inside or remove leftovers as soon as your pet finishes eating. Do not approach a bear or attempt to block his escape route. Bears are extremely shy and will run from people if given the opportunity, but they can't see very well. Many reports of bear charging humans occur because the bear did not see the person and accidentally moved toward them.

The solution most people come up with to solve a nuisance bear problem is to trap and move the animal. First, this is not as easy as it sounds, and secondly, it is not a good solution for the bear or its new neighbors. The bear may be moved 50 miles or more and dumped out in a remote area that it has never seen before. Its chances of getting into trouble are better than ever before! It may move to the nearest house or state park and look for an easy handout or unprotected trash cans. Thus, DNR has successfully transferred a nuisance problem from one place to another. Being in unfamiliar territory, the bear is more likely to get killed by cars or poachers and is also subject to being chased out again by territorial adult male and female bears which already occupy the territory.

Even in the remotest areas, there are no longer any places where bears can be stocked into unoccupied bear habitat or far enough from the nearest house. If you are already faced with a nuisance bear problem, call your state DNR. They have more good advice and literature plus repellents and scare pistols. Remember that the best long-term solution is to remove the easy food source. There is plenty of food for bears in their natural habitat and they can find it easily. Bears and people can coexist peacefully if both follow the rules. The golden rule is **Please don't feed the bears!**

Are you afraid of bears? A healthy fear of bears is ok, but some folks get really carried away. If you are afraid to walk, jog, take out your garbage, or walk your dog because of bears, then maybe you need to learn more about black bears. You need to know that you have less chance of being injured by a bear than by bees, lightning, golf, tennis, fire ants, ticks, dogs, snakes, home accidents and auto accidents! The child killed by a bear near the Great Smoky Mountains National Park recently was only the second fatality caused by a black bear on national parks in U.S. history. Most bear experts think the whole incident was a real fluke. We may never know all the circumstances behind that incident. Luckily, no one in North Georgia or many other eastern states has ever been seriously injured by a bear.

Residents living in bear country need to learn about bears, not just fear them. Just like the saying goes, "Can't we all just get along?" The answer is *yes*! Everyone needs to work hard to keep the bears "wild." This is done by *not* providing them free meals in your yard or neighborhood. Treat bears with respect, and don't tolerate the feeding of bears in your neighborhood. When bears use bird feeders, garbage, or pet food, a conflict is instantly created between the homeowner and the bear. These "adversely trained" bears mean an eventual death sentence for the bear and a real pest for the entire neighborhood.

Meanwhile, if you should have a surprise bear encounter, do not panic and do not run. Back slowly away and make lots of noise. However, if the bear approaches you, stand your ground. Wave your arms above your head and yell. The bear will go away. Some bears with cubs are just like human mothers in that they will attempt to protect their cubs. Do not try to get close to the cubs! Sow bears pushed to the limit are prone to pop their jaws, raise the hair on their neck and make a loud "Woof." Some might even bluff charge, stopping 10 feet or more short of the intruder. They have no interest in eating anyone, just putting some distance between the intruder and their cubs.

Bears are not aggressive, evil creatures, nor are they cute, cuddly teddy bears either. They are wildlife–part of the forest and part of our lives. To live in or near bear country means learning to live with bears. It is not that difficult, and it should be considered a privilege!

DEER ACTIVITY PEAKS
IN NOVEMBER

November is the best time of year to observe, hunt or watch out for deer (all motorists need to be vigilant), as the peak of both breeding season and hunting season coincide. White-tailed deer were once nearly eliminated in Georgia and many other eastern states due to poaching and extensive habitat destruction, but through exhaustive restocking and wildlife management efforts, deer have been successfully restored to all of their former native range throughout Georgia. In fact, the population peaked at 1.4 million in 1997 and currently stands at nearly one million animals. Deer are a valuable natural, recreational, and economic resource in

Georgia, bringing in more than $900 million per year in hunting license fees, sporting equipment sales, hunting trip expenses and land leases. However, high deer densities in some localized areas have the potential to inflict significant damage to forestry, agricultural or horticultural crops, home gardens, ornamental shrubbery and their own woodland food supplies. But because deer are important both biologically and economically, management of their numbers requires serious consideration on multiple levels. Regulated hunting is the only effective way to control and manage deer populations. Coyotes are also becoming important predators on deer fawns, killing as many as 25-50 percent or more of newborn deer fawns in some areas. Ironically, they may be accomplishing a valuable deer population reduction service for landowners who grow gardens and ornamentals.

Scientific studies of white-tailed deer funded by sportsmen in the form of taxes on arms and ammunition over the past 70-plus years have provided much information on deer biology and behavior. For example, adult deer in the east weigh from 70 to 250 pounds, with bucks typically weighing more than does. Breeding season (called "the rut") extends from October to January and peaks in November. Deer ranges expand and movements increase greatly during the rut. This is good news for hunters but bad news for motorists! Gestation period for does is about 200 days. Newborn fawns are spotted and range from four to eight pounds. Most are born between May and July with a peak in June. For the first month or so, does spend very little time with fawns, hiding them for hours and returning to nurse them only four to six times in 24 hours. This tactic helps keep scent levels low so predators are not attracted to newborns. However, coyotes, bears and bobcats have learned to search for fawns by sight (and faint scent) in likely bedding areas. Young fawns begin foraging on plants within a month, becoming much less vulnerable to predators, and are completely weaned from doe's milk in about three months.

Annual deer home range sizes vary from 150 acres to more than 1,200 acres with does having much smaller ranges than bucks. Smaller ranges also are found in higher deer populations and in better deer habitat. As most hunters are well aware, deer have a crepuscular activity pattern, meaning they are most active around dawn and dusk. Motorists must be aware of this pattern also!

Although most hunters think in terms of bucks, it is management of the doe segment of the herd that determines most all of the differences in deer population size. For example, depending on the food supply and the total deer population, does can produce twins, singles, or not bear any fawns at all. If births exceed the total death rate from hunting and other causes in any particular year, then the population increases. Eventually, the population reaches a size where it exceeds the available food supply ("carrying capacity") of the land resulting in lower birth rates, poor antler development, lower body weights and eventually a lower population as the remaining food supply is permanently damaged. Consequently, deer herds are the result of a complex interaction of hunting pressure, food supply, population size, births, deaths, movements, weather, and past history. Hunting is the only tried-and-true method for managing deer populations in order to reach desired deer herd densities in good condition.

Antler development is important to many hunters and deer observers. Buck antler development is controlled by age, nutrition, and genetics. However, in most places, genetics do not appear to be an important controlling factor because the genetic composition of deer is good. For example, the restocking effort in Georgia included three major sources: Georgia coastal islands, Wisconsin and Texas. The resulting "blend" of genetics from these far-removed sources has resulted in some of the best antler characteristics in the entire Southeast.

Consequently, for most deer in Georgia and virtually every other eastern state, age is the single most limiting factor for antler development, followed by nutrition. Under heavy hunting pressure, bucks simply may not live long enough to produce large antlers as it takes three to six years for bucks to reach their maximum potential. Also, poor nutrition can occur when deer herds get too large and reduce quality or quantity of their food supply, resulting in poor antler growth.

Deer are our only native animals that routinely browse plants five feet above the ground. They eat about five pounds per day (dry weight) of hundreds of species of both native and non-native plants but have definite preferences for certain plants, fruits and nuts. Some of their favorites include Japanese honeysuckle, acorns, grapes, apples, persimmons, greenbrier, wheat, oats and clover. In the fall, deer appear to be concentrating most of the time on white oak acorns, clover and persimmons. Do not discount red oaks as a preferred fall food favorite (see the chapter on acorns).

November is a magical month for a lot of outdoor enthusiasts but especially hunters, because bucks are moving more than any other time of year. They are also chasing does, making scrapes and rubbing trees with their antlers to mark their territories. Their "sign" in the woods keeps hunters encouraged that bucks are nearby and helps them stay in the hunt even in cold and inclement weather. Most hunters will have a great hunt this fall whether they harvest a deer or not. It is just being out there quietly observing the best of nature that seems to mean the most. There is also something to be said for some fresh, high-quality venison and maybe a nice set of antlers to go along with it!

WINNING THE DEER WARS
IN YARD AND GARDEN!

Spring is mostly a fun and pleasant season here in North Georgia and the rest of the eastern states. We usually get plenty of rain to grow gardens and ornamental plants, and it is a beautiful time of year—with one possible exception. Everything we try to grow in our gardens and landscaping that tastes or looks good seems to get molested or gobbled up by those four-legged, four-stomached munching machines called white-tailed deer! And deer can consume forage at the rate of five pounds dry weight (15 pounds or more green weight) per deer per day! This scenario is very common across the eastern half of the country. After a long, hard winter of chasing squirrels away from bird feeders, the battle front changes to all out warfare in the garden, as we try to get a garden variety bean all the way to the freezer without it being devastated by marauding deer, groundhogs, beavers or rabbits. We all love to see these graceful critters around in the fall and winter, but they can quickly become pests in spring when vegetable gardens and new landscape plants spring up.

One of the most common and frustrating problems is deer eating our expensive landscape shrubbery or our favorite garden vegetables. Those rascals dearly love tender stuff like peas, beans, okra, peppers, squash, corn, watermelons, pumpkins, fruit trees, redtips, azaleas, hostas, rhododendron, various other nursery stock and almost every other valuable food or ornamental plant which has been fertilized. Even fertilized pine trees have been known to sustain a lot of deer damage in some places and some years!

Remedies, of course, vary with the type of crop, its location, value, and the severity of damage. For long-term protection of valuable crops, there is nothing better than electric fencing to keep out deer and even rabbits and groundhogs. These fences, made up of one- to five-strands of polytape (electroplastic) wire, are an expensive initial investment but can protect a valuable orchard or vegetable garden for 10 to 20 years. Using quality materials, a small, one- to three-strand electric fence can be installed for $0.30 to $0.40 per foot. If only one strand is used, it needs to be 30 inches above the ground. Before initial operation, it is important to mix a slurry of peanut butter with a small amount of cooking oil and dab it on the fence at three- to six-foot intervals. When curious animals show up to sniff and taste the peanut butter, the wire will deliver a memorable shock to the nose or tongue. Usually, one touch is enough to keep deer out for a long time, perhaps even years.

There is a commercial product available from www.cabelas.com and other websites for about $40 to exclude deer by sight and smell called Plot Saver Deer Barrier System, which is a one-acre kit composed of absorbent ribbon and liquid deer repellent. Buy 39-inch fiberglass stakes and you are in business for a reasonable price.

Another variation for a fence is a simple cotton rope soaked in commercial deer repellents (such as Hinder, Deer Away, Deer Stopper, Deer Off, Liquid Fence and others) and strung 30 inches above the ground to enclose the garden. Re-apply repellent to the rope at two-week intervals (or more frequently in rainy weather) to reinforce the odor. See specific fence materials and instructions at the end of this chapter.

Other methods to keep deer out of gardens and shrubbery include scare devices and repellents applied directly to plants. Most of the time these are effective if used frequently, interchangeably, and persistently. Some common techniques which work well for a few days include scarecrows (moved every other day), mylar balloons, pie tins, transistor radios, flashing lights, dogs, dirty socks, ballcaps or T-shirts with fresh human odor, strips of flagging tape or cloth, or a simple line of string. These methods work temporarily, especially if used inter-changeably or in combination with fencing or repellents.

Repellents can be effective over the short-term and include both commercial varieties and home remedies. One of the best home remedies to repel deer contains four raw eggs, a couple of ounces of carefully strained garlic juice, a few drops of dishwashing liquid, and a gallon of lukewarm water sprayed directly on the vulnerable vegetation, flowers, shrubs, etc. This imparts a sulfurous odor that is effective in low rainfall periods. I have personally used this solution on flowers and it works for a few days or until the next rain! Another temporary repellent is bars of motel-sized soap with holes punched in the wrappers. String these about four feet above the ground from the limbs of fruit trees, shrubbery, or stakes placed around the edges of a garden. This has proven effective especially to protect individual trees from browsing.

Another product that works well is an organic fertilizer called Milorganite which is available in 50-pound bags. It is the byproduct of highly treated human solid waste and has a faint sulfurous odor which will repel deer for 30 to 45 days. Application rate is 250 lbs/acre. I would not use it in the garden, but it would be appropriate for individual ornamental plants. Apply on the ground over the root system about ½ to one inch deep. Re-apply every 30 days during the growing season.

There are also a wide variety of commercial repellents which can be purchased from garden supply or hardware stores, catalogs, and orchardists. One of the best of these in recent tests has proven to be Hinder (or Fertilome Deer & Rabbit Repellent), an ammonia-based liquid which is relatively inexpensive. These are the only commercial repellents approved for spraying directly on food crops during the active growing season. Be sure to read and follow the label. They can be applied directly to the foliage of vegetable and field crops, gardens, ornamentals, fruit trees, and nursery stock. Another effective tool is several variations of motion-activated sprinklers which quickly spray water on the deer and a host of other critters. They do not like this and will quickly move away.

Georgia DNR has a booklet available for free to the public entitled *Controlling Deer Damage in Georgia.* Go to http://www. georgiawildlife.com/node/253. I wrote most of this booklet a few years ago. State DNR wildlife biologists or your county agricultural extension agent also have helpful remedies and suggestions for almost any wildlife problem around the home or garden. Meanwhile, good luck with the war on munching machines, and remember that these are the same animals you love to have around in the fall and winter. The life of an outdoor enthusiast would surely be dull without them!

A Solar Powered Electric Fence to Exclude Deer (for ¼ acre)

Materials:

- 450 feet 1½-inch wide, high-visibility polytape electric fence wire
- 40 insulated fence posts 48 inches tall with insulators
- solar powered fence charger
- peanut butter (one small jar) & one tablespoon cooking oil

Instructions:

Install fence posts one-foot deep at about 10-foot intervals. Attach polytape fence wire at 30 inches height to insulators on posts and to charger. Mix peanut butter and oil to form a slurry. Dab on polytape at three to six foot intervals. Turn on charger.

A Simple Deer Repellent Fence (for ¼ acre)

Materials:

- 450 feet 3/8-inch cotton rope
- 40 fiberglass fence posts 48 inches tall
- Liquid Fence deer repellent concentrate, one quart
- old cooler or bucket and plastic gloves

Instructions:

Install fence posts one-foot deep at about 10-foot intervals. Soak rope in repellent/water solution in bucket/cooler for five or 10 minutes. Attach rope at 30-inch height to fence posts. Re-apply repellent solution to rope with spray bottle as needed at two- to four-week intervals.

"ORPHANED DEER FAWNS"

B eginning in May and throughout the month of June and into July, the forests and fields of North Georgia and the eastern half of the United States are full of cute, spotted, newborn deer fawns bedded down and curled up in balls all alone waiting for their mamas to return. Don't try to be a Good Samaritan and "rescue" a fawn. For sure, don't take a fawn home with you! If you already have and haven't kept it over 48 hours, put it back! What might appear to be a tiny, helpless, orphaned or abandoned fawn is really a normal fawn with a normal mother who only visits the fawn five or six short times per day to nurse it. What about dad? He is nowhere near, off with his buck buddies growing antlers and leaving all domestic duties to the doe. This is nature's way for the tiny fawn's best survival chances.

Read on.

For its first month of life, a fawn instinctively spends 90 percent of its time alone, away from its mother, curled up in a nearly invisible ball hiding from predators. It will not move, not even twitch an ear, unless a predator virtually steps on it. This approach is not cruel and it works! The doe intentionally avoids the immediate area of the fawn to reduce scent and keep from attracting predators such as dogs, coyotes, bears or bobcats. Lying motionless in heavy cover, the fawn has two big advantages: 1) It emits virtually no scent, which might attract predators, and 2) Its russet (orange-brown) coat with about 300 white spots is a natural camouflage pattern that enables them to hide virtually unseen. This strategy on average allows about 50 to 75 percent of newborns to survive to six months of age and older.

The strategy is almost foolproof, except for one big hitch. When well-meaning people come along and find the fawn all by itself, the trouble begins. Although mother doe is nearby, our Jane Do-gooder does not know this, and she stumbles upon a tiny "orphaned" fawn in the woods behind her house. For their first 10 days of life, fawns are easy to catch and that's what happens to this fawn—it gets caught and brought home. Of course, the first thing she does is feed it. Newborn fawns look like they are starving to death even when they are in tip-top shape. Even if fed the proper formula, chances are good that it will develop the scours (diarrhea), get seriously dehydrated and die. Under the very best human care (veterinarians included), studies have shown that about 50 percent of all rescued captive deer fawns die. Suppose the do-gooder decides to call the DNR wildlife biologist for advice. She wants the biologist to come get the fawn and put it in a place where someone will raise it to live happily ever after. Sorry, there is no such place. The zoos, game farms, research centers, nature centers, and parks are all full of deer. Most want to get rid of their own surplus deer, certainly not take on another one. The fawn can't be raised by hand and turned loose in the real world because they remain forever tame and vulnerable to predators, people and vehicles. Besides, tame bucks in the rut create a real danger to people. Attacks on people by tame bucks are not rare, and they actually happen frequently in deer research facilities in October, November or December when bucks are rutting. Also, turning a tame deer loose in the wild is not fair to the animal. They have no survival skills and end up getting killed by coyotes, dogs, fences or automobiles.

What to do? Don't pick up any fawns unless you are absolutely sure the mother is dead, for example a fawn lying next to its dead mother on the side of the road. If you have already made the mistake, call your state DNR immediately and report it. If it has been less than 48 hours since the fawn was picked up, it can be carefully replaced in the same locality and the mother will likely find it. The old wives tale that a doe won't accept a fawn with human scent on it is pure baloney! If it has been longer than this, then you will likely be asked to bring the fawn to a nearby wildlife rehabilitator. There are many trained licensed rehabilitators with fawn-raising experience all over the country. This is not a good fate for the fawn, but it is probably better than nothing. Under no circumstances should anyone attempt to raise the fawn themselves, as it is illegal, very difficult and unproductive for both the do-gooder and the fawn.

There are literally millions of newborn fawns quietly lying alone and still in the woods and fields of every state that harbors whitetails from May through July. That is the way Mother Nature meant for it to be for a fawn's own best survival chances. It works! Remember, you can't fool Mother Nature! Also remember, no one is more qualified to raise a fawn than mama doe herself.

ACORNS: NUMBER ONE
WILDLIFE FOOD

W hen it comes to annual acorn production, oak trees of all species are on a roller-coaster ride . Due to energy cycles, droughts, poor pollination and spring frosts during blooming, the crop can vary from virtually zero to maximum production and every number in between. I ran the same 10- to 15-mile acorn survey route for almost 30 years in the north Georgia mountains. Elevations ranged from about 1,600 to about 3,400 feet above sea level thus representing climate conditions and oak species as far as 1,000 miles north. I conducted the survey by scanning a total of about 150 oak tree crowns with binoculars in early September, then assigning a whole number rating from 0 to 10 to each tree. Averages of 0.00-

1.99 indicated a poor crop, 2.00-3.00 rated fair and above 3.0 rated good. Poor crops were totally consumed by early November, fair crops by early December, and good crops lasted well into winter.

Acorns lying on the ground through the fall aren't necessarily viable. Many of the nuts you see on the ground are rotten– damaged by weevils, birds, squirrels and weather– and consequently passed over by deer and other mammals whose keen sense of smell can detect the rot inside. With wild turkeys and other birds, it is likely their excellent eyesight detects the tiny weevil hole. It is much harder for people to evaluate the soundness of acorns. Some have a tiny hole where a female weevil bored through the hull and deposited eggs that hatched into worms (larvae), which feed on the nut inside. One way to find out is to place acorns in a bucket of water. Damaged acorns will float, sound acorns sink. Finally, a small pair of pliers can be used to crush the hull and see for yourself once and for all whether the nut is still good or not. Do this on five or 10 nuts under one tree to determine if any sound acorns are still left and deer and other wildlife are still visiting that tree. By early to mid-November, most if not all white oaks are finished dropping all their nuts, and the rotten unconsumed leftovers are the only ones left on the ground to tell the story.

One potential scenario is a very good year for white oak acorn production and a very poor one for red oaks. This can be good news for deer and squirrel hunters if they can find the remaining productive white oaks or an isolated red oak still dropping nuts, as the red oak group drops longer and later than the white oak group. There are at least 54 oak species native to the United States, and they are widely distributed over most of the eastern part of the country. They thrive at different altitudes and in many different soil types. White oak group species in north Georgia include white, chestnut and post oaks. Red oak species include northern red, southern red, scarlet, black, blackjack and water oaks. Progressing further north to New England and the Upper Midwest, the oak species include bur, white, swamp white and chestnut of the white oak group and northern red, black and scarlet of the red oak group. All are valuable to wildlife.

Acorns rate a position at the top of the wildlife food list with usage by over 100 species of animals including deer, wild turkey, bears, squirrels, raccoons and many more mammals and birds. White-tailed deer use of acorns has been reported as high as 52 percent of their diet in Texas and up to 50 percent in Missouri and Alabama. Acorns contain a relatively low protein level (6 percent) but are high in fat and carbohydrates at maturity in the fall when deer and other critters need fat to over-winter in a healthy condition.

Acorns have been repeatedly tied to deer abundance, reproduction, buck harvest numbers, body weight, antler development and even over- winter survival. Deer populations exposed to acorn failure followed by a harsh winter are subject to mortality in the north Georgia mountains and further north.

One study done in North Carolina showed average production of well-developed acorns ranged from 6,600 per acre per year to 94,600 per acre per year. The quality of acorns is as important as the quantity produced. On average, only two of three acorns were fully developed. Of these, the number of sound and undamaged acorns varied from only 11 percent to 73 percent. Hence the detective work needed as described in the first paragraph. Production of sound acorns on 2/3-acre plots ranged from zero to 145,400! Acorns were damaged by insects (mostly weevils), birds and squirrels, and were imperfectly developed, deformed or aborted. Late spring frosts, poor bloom, and lack of pollination are other important factors affecting the size of the acorn crop each year.

Major differences between the white and red oak groups are that the white oak group blooms and produces a mature acorn in the same year while red oaks bloom and produce a mature acorn in the second year. The white oak group has rounded leaf margins (lobes) contrasted to pointed lobes with a bristle on the tips of red oak leaves. There are other important differences too numerous to detail here. Due to lower tannic acid content, white oak acorns are generally more preferred by deer and other wildlife than red oaks. Sawtooth oak, a non-native red oak is a notable exception to this, reported to be equal to white oak in palatability. This difference in palatability among groups can be very important to deer and squirrel hunters trying to pinpoint movements as acorns disappear gradually throughout the fall.

The importance of oak species diversity is unmistakable since red and white oaks (probably due to the one year difference in time to maturity) rarely fail in the same year. Consequently, the two groups often buffer each other year after year, mostly preventing a total failure of both groups in the same year. This is important because of the wildly fluctuating nature of acorn production.

Wildlife managers manage oak stands for large crown diameter and air movement around crowns. Peak production age for oaks is usually 50 to100 years of age. Managers select cut dominant trees to release productive oaks from surrounding competition such as hickory, white pine, gums, poplar or maple.

Finally, while not proven by research, fertilization of individual trees may help increase acorn production. A complete fertilizer (such as 10-10-10) broadcast underneath mature oaks evenly out to the drip line at the rate of one pound per inch of diameter at breast height (DBH) in early spring may increase acorn production. Individual oaks located around lawns, pastures, croplands, and other fertilized areas have long been noted for heavier, more consistent acorn production, although other factors (such as fewer insects or better air circulation around crowns) may also be involved with the increased production of these oaks. Genetics is also a huge factor which can "program" individual oaks to be poor or heavy producers and everything in between. I saw this genetically controlled production of individual trees clearly on my acorn survey route. Some individual trees bore heavy crops of acorns every year while others produced poorer crops only once every three to five years.

Though inconsistent and unpredictable, acorns make up a very important component of fall and winter diet of deer and 100 other wildlife species, especially where diversity of oak species among both white and red oak groups is high. Although white oaks as a whole are more palatable to deer, red oaks are more consistent producers in the long run. Both are extremely important components of a well-managed forest program.

WILD HOGS:

GOOD, BAD OR UGLY

Much to the delight of some big-game hunters and much to the infuriation and frustration of most landowners and managers, wild hogs are on the increase in the Southeast and nationwide. They are literally a wildlife manager's worst nightmare, and if you don't believe it can be all that bad, keep reading.

Domestic hogs were first introduced to the Southeastern United States in the 1500s by Spanish explorer Fernando DeSoto. These original invaders were eventually joined in more modern times by "Russian" or Eurasian wild boar, which were turned loose intentionally or escaped accidentally from enclosures. Add to this escapees from farms, and the genetics of different hog populations range from pure domestic stock to almost pure Eurasian stock and everything in between.

"Feral hogs" (feral meaning escaped and now free-ranging) is a more accurate name for wild hogs which are normally considered domestic but live in a wild state. As referenced above, they are now often mixed with "Russian" boar that were accidentally or intentionally turned loose in parts of the Southeast years ago.

No longer exclusively a Southeastern problem, feral hogs (*Sus scrofa*) now exist in the wild in parts of Nebraska, Kansas, Missouri, Michigan, Wisconsin, Indiana, Ohio, New Hampshire and New York as well as other mid-South, Western and Southwestern states. Texas and California are covered up with them.

Wild hogs are fiercely competitive invasive exotics that are more destructive, dangerous and controversial than coyotes. They are not even considered a "game animal" or "wildlife" in most states and therefore are only marginally referenced in state laws and regulations as enforced by natural resource and wildlife management agencies. The bottom line is that feral hogs are usually considered the property of the landowner upon whose ground they are currently standing.

The purpose of this article is threefold: (1) to detail the good, bad, and ugly sides of feral hogs; (2) to explain why they are increasing in Georgia and other states, and (3) to explain when and how to control hogs.

The Good News

The good news for some hunters is obvious. Another "big game animal" makes life more interesting for the hunter and can fill the freezer with tasty meat. There is a downside to be aware of, and that is diseases such as swine brucellosis and pseudorabies. Humans can contract brucellosis but not pseudorabies. Even though both diseases are rare in Georgia and other states, proper precautions should be practiced. Wear disposable plastic gloves when dressing or cleaning wild hogs. Avoid direct skin contact with blood and organs. As soon as possible, wash hands with soap and hot water after dressing hogs. One more precaution is in order: always cook pork (wild or domestic) to a minimum of 165 degrees Fahrenheit to avoid the nematode parasite that causes trichinosis in people. Just like the diseases mentioned above, this parasite is also rarely found in wild hog populations.

All that aside, what could be more interesting than to go on a buck, bear, and boar hunt in the Georgia mountains and have a good chance at bagging any of the three? There is something extra stimulating about hunting hogs because of the great abundance of sign they make in the woods in the form of rooting, wallows, and tracks. However, right here is where the good news ends with hogs.

The Bad News

The bad news is cause for much concern. Non-native (exotic) hogs are invasive and compete directly for food with over 100 species of our native wildlife including deer, turkeys, squirrels, grouse, bears, songbirds, and small mammals. Acorns from over 50 species of oaks are an obvious food in high demand and especially important to all these species, but the competition doesn't end there. Hogs are extremely omnivorous and eat a little of everything including grass and clover (planted in food plots for deer), fruits, roots, insects, grubs, salamanders, and small mammals. They will even kill and eat young deer fawns! The overall relationship is clear: more hogs equal less of all other wildlife species, especially deer and turkeys. Strong scientific evidence already points to the hog/deer negative relationship.

The Ugly News

The last straw regarding hogs is the ugly angle. It's the habitat destruction caused by rooting. Hogs do not discriminate about when and where they root. Rooting is common in agricultural crops, fields and forests. I recently saw a five-acre deer food plot turned over from one end to the other by hog rooting. It does not end there. Hogs have been known to disrupt entire ecosystems including endangered plants and animals. No wonder the U.S. Forest Service and state wildlife agencies both take a dim view of hogs on national forests and state lands. The problem is not by any means confined to Georgia but is a chronic problem in the entire Southeast. It is also rapidly getting worse in the Midwest and Northeast.

Reproduction and Movements

This brings up an important question – where are all these hogs coming from? There is no doubt that hogs are increasing nationwide. Their home ranges stretch from 6 to 12 miles in length, and some researchers even claim they are semi-nomadic, with the potential to completely leave one range in search of another. They are easily expanding their range by prolific reproduction.

Sows can breed as early as six months of age, and they can bear two litters per year with up to 13 pigs per litter. This rate of reproduction falls just a little short of the rate exhibited by rabbits and far exceeds the one or two fawns per adult doe per year. It is totally unmatched by any other large mammal and can lead to a local population more than doubling in one year.

These movements and reproductive rates are enough on their own to lead to population expansion, but there's yet another factor – they are also being stocked illegally on both public and private lands by misinformed hog enthusiasts. Besides being illegal in most areas, the practice is ignorant and destructive. While hogs may be desired on one landowner's property, they will not remain there for long. Illegal stocking is no doubt to blame for many of the scattered "outlier" populations now seen across the United States. The "hog hunters" who do this are the same folks who complain about the lack of deer in areas invaded by illegally stocked hogs. Is there a connection? Guaranteed! More hogs equals fewer deer and other wildlife!

The Solution

What's the solution? Keep hunting pressure high and remove as many hogs as possible. This is obviously some more good news for hunters. Hog hunting restrictions or regulations can vary from one state to the next. For example, in north Georgia, the only restrictions on hog hunting are those which apply to the Chattahoochee National Forest (CNF) and all WMAs on or off of CNF. On these lands, hogs may be taken with archery equipment during archery deer season, with deer weapons during firearms deer season, with turkey weapons during turkey season, and with small game weapons during small game season. On special hog hunts, specified in the WMA regulations, big game weapons may be used, and hunter orange may be required. There is no daily bag limit unless otherwise specified. Hunting and WMA licenses are required. Electronic hog calls are permitted, but you may not hunt at night. Hog populations can be spotty and somewhat nomadic. Check with your state DNR for hunting regulations.

On private lands in Georgia, hog hunting is mostly unrestricted. Here again, this varies from state to state. There are no firearms, season, or daily bag limit restrictions for taking feral hogs! However, in north Georgia, no hunting over bait during deer season and no hunting from a vehicle is allowed. You can hunt at night with a light which is carried on the person, affixed to a helmet or hat, or part of a belt system worn by a hunter.

There are special permits available from DNR which allow these practices such as hunting from a vehicle and hunting over bait and others under certain conditions. Outside of Georgia, check with your state wildlife agency as hog hunting rules and regulations will likely be different than those above.

Scouting for hog sign is easier than scouting for deer sign. Hogs are notorious rooters and often turn over large areas of forest and agricultural land. Rooting usually consists of large irregular areas where turf, dirt and humus are turned over or long wavy, wandering lines of ruffled up leaves where hogs put their long noses on the ground and push ahead sniffing for food under the leaves. The number one hog food in the fall is acorns. If acorns are already totally consumed, then hog sign can be found in grassy openings, creek bottoms, swamps or white pines.

Winter is a good time to hog hunt because of the gap between deer and turkey hunting season. If you do bring home the bacon, all of us and all of wildlife will benefit from fewer invaders in the forests and fields!

For more detailed information on wild hogs, go to: www.feralhogs.tamu.edu/files/2010/05/Feral-Hogs-in-Georgia.pdf for a free booklet. This publication also has plans for building your own hog traps. You can also obtain a wealth of information from the internet by googling "wild hog traps."

Coyotes: Bad News for Wildlife and Pets

S o you heard some coyotes howling or maybe even saw a coyote the other day? They sound almost like wolves howling and are most often heard at dusk when they emerge from their den to begin hunting. What kind of threat do they pose to you, your children or your pets? What about our native wildlife species? Read on.

Coyotes are not at all rare these days and are found in all lower 48 states and all of Georgia's 159 counties! They were released illegally in this state by fox hunters and also moved into Georgia on their own about 40 years ago by moving in from west to east through Tennessee and Alabama. In the North, they did the same thing in a wave from Minnesota all the way to New England.

How could that possibly be, you say, we hardly ever see one? Despite being common wherever they exist, coyotes are shy, secretive, elusive and for the most part nocturnal. Glimpses of coyotes are rare and fleeting. Despite being common near my property, I have only seen two on separate occasions in the past year, but my daughter saw four together crossing our driveway at midnight in the fall of 2011! At a distance, they are often mistaken for dogs, gray foxes or wolves (believe me, there are no wolves in the wild in Georgia).

Coyotes are usually a blended color of gray mixed with a reddish tint but show great variation in color ranging from pure gray to solid black. Some northern coyotes, as a result of crossbreeding with gray wolves or domestic dogs, weigh up to 50 pounds or more. The Georgia record weight is a male recorded at 40 pounds, but average weights here are 30 to 35 pounds (larger than a 15-lb. fox and much smaller than a 150- lb. gray wolf). Their total length is three to 3 ½ feet including a long bushy tail. Distinguishing features include upright pointed ears and a long-legged or stiff-legged appearance. They often run with a stiff-legged bounce and can run up to 40 mph in short spurts.

They use a makeshift den to raise their litter of four to seven pups born in March and April every year. Dens can occur in holes in steep banks, underneath uprooted trees, rock crevices, underbrush, gullies or enlarged fox or groundhog holes. Pups are weaned in about six weeks but often remain together with the adults until late summer or early fall. Coyote home range size varies greatly with males usually ranging much farther than females. One study in Arkansas showed an average home range of 13 square miles for males and five for females.

Coyote populations are usually not very high but appear to be increasing. When coyotes first become established in an area, the initial impact is often the decline or demise of the red fox population. Surprisingly, neither the red fox nor the coyote are native to the eastern states, but the gray fox and red wolf are native. The red wolf was declared extinct in the wild in 1980. In 1987, the U. S. Fish and Wildlife Service bred enough red wolves in captivity to begin a restoration program with four wolf pairs on Alligator River National Wildlife Refuge in northeastern North Carolina. Since then, the experimental population has expanded to include three national wildlife refuges, state-owned lands, and private property, spanning a total of 1.5 million acres. Currently, over 100 red wolves roam their native habitat in five northeastern North Carolina counties. The biggest concern is cross breeding with coyotes.

Soon after the coyote takeover of the red fox niche, several factors can begin limiting coyote numbers. Diseases and parasites commonly found in coyotes are distemper, hepatitis, parvovirus, mange, and heartworms. Much rarer diseases in coyotes are rabies and tularemia. All of these can control coyote numbers and keep them fairly moderate or low. It is also legal in most states to shoot coyotes at any time. Deer hunters and farmers shoot a few every year but most coyotes are so elusive that the great majority escape any form of attempted control with guns. Moreover, they are very difficult to trap and rarely does one get road- killed.

Coyotes are feared and hated by many people because of their reputation as killers. For the most part, their predatory impacts are exaggerated especially when it comes to prey the same size or larger. Also, coyotes usually hunt alone but more recently some have learned to hunt in pairs or small family packs when stalking larger prey. Coyote diets mostly consist of mice, rats, chipmunks, squirrels, rabbits, insects, carrion (dead animals), garbage, persimmons, watermelons, other fruit, nuts, and poultry. However, they are opportunistic omnivores which can occasionally kill adult deer that may be temporarily debilitated by fawn birth or are injured or sick. They can catch and kill young deer fawns up to about a month old, wild turkeys, small goats, sheep, house cats and small dogs. This last list usually makes up a smaller percentage of their diet except in June or July when newborn fawns are abundant.

They are commonly blamed for more mischief that is really caused by free-ranging dogs. One study done by Georgia DNR a few years ago kept track of coyote complaints investigated by their personnel in the field for over a 10-year period. More than 60 percent of complaints did not involve coyotes but were caused by some other animal (mostly dogs). Of the remaining 40 percent, coyotes were often implicated in feeding on a dead carcass but not really involved in the actual kill. These included sheep, goats, cattle, poultry, and ducks. Still born calves are a good example and so are calves killed or maimed by dogs and later found by coyotes. Of domestic livestock, chickens and goats appear to be the most vulnerable to coyote predation. Electric or tall conventional fencing may help solve most of the problems here.

The other real worry is protecting domestic pets such as house cats and small dogs. If you value your pets, do not let them roam free in the woods, especially at night! Your family cat that came up missing last year may have been killed by a coyote!

Finally, there is little reason to fear for your own safety, or that of your children. It is quite rare for coyotes to act aggressively or docile toward people. If one acts this way and also becomes active and commonly sighted during daylight hours, it is likely sick from a disease such as rabies or distemper. Kill it, if possible, or report it to Animal Control or DNR.

Inoculating all pets for rabies and the other canine diseases such as distemper, hepatitis, leptospirosis and parvovirus is highly recommended. The only direct danger to humans is the remote chance of rabies transmitted by a bite or scratch from a coyote. Meanwhile, the howling of a family of coyotes at night may raise the hair on the back of your neck but really should not be anything serious to worry about except for the small pet issue. It is simply a family group announcing and proclaiming their territory to all other coyote families in the area. Coyotes are here to stay and we can learn to live with them if we take necessary precautions with cats and small dogs.

Note: Chili, our dachshund male, who is featured in A Dog-Eat-Dog World chapter, was recently attacked and killed by coyotes only about 100 yards from our house.

STRANGE CRITTERS

The forests and fields of the eastern half of our country and north Georgia are full of mythical and strange creatures according to many folks including hunters, hikers, bird watchers, photographers, bikers, horse riders, property owners and many others who enjoy the outdoors. I know because I spent parts of a 30-year career as a senior wildlife biologist with Georgia DNR, Wildlife Resources Division, Game Management Section, answering questions about strange wildlife sightings and investigating some of them. They came mostly from my area of responsibility, a 16- county area in the northeastern corner of the state tucked between three bordering state lines.

Sometimes they trickled in over the phones, sometimes they were reported in person in the Gainesville DNR office, sometimes reported in person in the field...from a country store to a Wildlife Management Area deer hunt. They amounted to hundreds per year. The strange-critter sightings crank up heavily in the spring, go strong through fall, then calm down in winter as both people and animal activity slows down.

The furry list of what is really out there is long and includes deer, beavers, muskrats, groundhogs, foxes, coyotes, skunks, raccoons, weasels, mink, otters, bobcats, house cats, dogs and black bears. The list of reported species that are not likely out there is shorter and includes panthers, cougars, pumas, mountain lions, wolves, wolverines, badgers, ring-tailed coatis, Tasmanian devils and wompus cats (whatever that is). There are cases of internal mistaken identity when one native species is mistaken for another. Then there are external or crossover mistaken identity when a native animal is mistaken for a species that is not actually out there.

Internal mistakes involve species in the first group that is sure enough really out there and go something like this when the phone rings…"Hello, can I help you?"

"Yes, you have to do something, it's awful" said the truck driver who just drove 50 miles from Blairsville to Gainesville through the mountains on Hwy 129 in March.

"What do you mean?" I said.

"I just saw 19 orphaned bear cubs on the side of the road out there eating grass without any mama bears with them at all. Someone is killing all the mama bears and leaving baby bears out there alone to starve to death. You gotta do something!" "Hmmm, what color are the bear cubs?" I ask.

"They are brown and only weigh about eight or 10 pounds, they'll starve!"

"Sir, have you ever heard of groundhogs? I think what you saw may be groundhogs eating the green grass on the roadsides in early spring after they awaken hungry from hibernation."

"Oh no," said the truck driver, "I know what a ground hog is but these were brown bear cubs!"

"Sir, we don't have any brown bears in Georgia, only black ones." "Well" he continued, "These were dark brown."

Knowing there was no way of convincing the guy, I said "Ok, I'll have someone check on it." But obviously, I didn't. This was the typical internal native species identity crossover, because both black bears and groundhogs do really exist in North Georgia and most of the eastern half of the country.

There was another incident in Hall County several years ago. The same call could originate anywhere in the eastern states where bears exist. Hall County Dispatch called and said there was a bear cub up a tree in someone's front yard. Deputies and firefighters were on the scene, and so was a large crowd of people. Sounded bad to me. Where was mama bear and what would she do to get her cub back? I loaded my dart gun and sped to the scene as did wildlife technician Walt Sutton from the other direction.

We arrived at about the same time, scanning the horizon for any sign of mama bear. It was a mob scene with about 50 people gathered in a front yard. Deputies cleared us a path through the crowd to the base of a big oak tree. About 30 feet up in a crotch was a little brown ball of fur with beady black eyes and tiny ears, staring down at all the commotion. Walt and I looked at each other rolling our eyes simultaneously and choking back a big chuckle. We pulled a fireman and deputy aside and stated matter of factly that the treed animal was an 8-lb. groundhog not a 20-lb. bear cub. They did not believe us. The deputy said "How could he get up there?"

"Chased by a dog," I said. "They have sharp claws and can climb better than you think." I said the only way I could prove it to him would be to shoot the little furry ball with this big old dart, and that would not be pretty. If General Beauregard Lee survived the heavy dose of drug in the dart, he would not survive the fall from the tree.

We did not want to embarrass the officers and fire-fighters. We suggested getting all the people cleared out of there so the "cub" could come down by himself and go find "mama bear." They did, and that's what happened…or so everyone thought.

More common are the external mistaken identity crossovers where an animal on the real existence list is mistaken for one that is not. A few years ago, I took a call from the Forsyth County side of Lake Lanier, and the caller said "You have to come over here and get rid of this badger!"

"Badger?" I said, "Are you sure?"

"Oh yes" was the answer, "I watch him go in and out of his hole, he is brown with a short tail and sometimes flattens out on the ground or stands up on his back legs."

"Does he have a black mask like a raccoon and big long claws?" I inquire.

"No, not really" was the answer "but he weighs about 25-lbs. and can climb trees when my dog gets after him."

"Does he have long flat front teeth like a beaver, little beady eyes and a short flat furry tail?"

"Why yes!" says the caller. "Ma'am, I believe what you have is probably a 10-lb. groundhog, not a 25-lb. badger! The nearest badger to north Georgia is about 1,000 miles away and if you had a badger, he would tear your dog to pieces, not just go up a tree."

By the way, as a rule, every critter caller exaggerates the weight of the critter!

These true stories pale in comparison to the frequent cougar, black panther and wolf sightings that spread fear and terror throughout north Georgia and many other neighborhoods across the country as these predators threaten to eat pets, children and old folks right off the front porch! Stay tuned for the next chapter as we explore the list of predatory big critters with big sharp teeth that may or may not really exist in the forests of this corner of Georgia, or most any other corner in the East.

STRANGE CRITTERS
WITH BIG, SHARP TEETH

G ot any panthers, pumas, cougars, mountain lions, lynx or wolves? You laugh? Reported sightings of these big, mean, toothy predators are quite common in Georgia and almost everywhere else people live in close proximity to forests. In the last chapter, I discussed mistaken identities between bears, groundhogs and badgers. This chapter gets even better–or scarier–as the creatures get bigger and more mysterious but less likely to even exist in the wilds of Georgia or any other eastern state!

First off, panthers, pumas, cougars and mountain lions are four names for the same big cat-the eastern cougar-which used to live here over 100 years ago but became extinct due to persecution from the early settlers and loss of woodland habitat. The nearest big cats now are the Florida panthers in south Florida, and these are extremely rare with only 100 to 120 left in the wild. Surprisingly, there was one killed in Troup County in west central Georgia in November 2008. It was a male weighing 140 pounds. Genetic testing confirmed that it was for sure a Florida panther who had moved over 650 miles north of the established south Florida population. Movements of this nature and length are quite rare! Until this killing, there had been no concrete evidence of the big cats in Georgia since the early 1970s when a plaster cast was made of a track in the northwestern part of the state and verified as a cougar by the Smithsonian Institute. There was of course not enough information or evidence to speculate how that big cat got there and whether it was wild or escaped from captivity.

In the early 1990s, the U.S. Fish & Wildlife Service and Florida Fish and Wildlife decided to stock a few sterile (fixed by veterinarians) western cougars in north Florida complete with radio collars. It was a pilot program to see if they could eventually stock actual Florida panthers and extend their range northward. The experiment eventually failed as the big cats got into big conflicts with civilization by killing livestock, getting run over on the highways and being shot.

One of these big cats moved over 150 miles north until it was near Augusta, Georgia. They tracked his radio signal, treed him, shot him with a tranquilizer dart and brought him back to Florida. Not long after that, they ended up catching all of the remaining cats and abandoning the total effort. There was just too much conflict with people and their civilized world. It was a wildlife experiment that failed and cost taxpayers a lot of money.

It was similar to another failed experiment with wide-ranging, big predators that occurred more recently with the red wolf stocking in The Great Smoky Mountains National Park in southeastern Tennessee. After about seven years, what was left of them got picked up by the Feds, and the program was quietly abandoned. Besides the wolves getting into trouble on private lands, there was very low pup survival due to coyote predation and diseases as well as a distinct probability of these wolves crossbreeding with coyotes. By the way, none of these wolves (all carrying radio collars around their necks) ever moved into Georgia. Red wolves were native here but were exterminated well over 100 years ago just like the panthers. These places like the Great Smoky Mountains and north Florida flatwoods appear remote enough, but they are just fragmented forested rural areas, too civilized for big wide-ranging predators and full of people, cars, highways, fences, dogs, cattle and big trouble for big cats and wolves. The Feds had to find out, and they did! However, both of these abandoned projects did serve to stimulate lots of sightings and reports in Georgia that were false, and totally unrelated to actual locations of any of the animals being monitored. Ah yes, human imaginations are a wonderful thing!

So, when people call and report a panther or a wolf, what are they really seeing? I don't know, but it could be coyotes (plenty of them around), bobcats, dogs, otters, house cats or bears. No lynx (close relative of a bobcat but bigger at about 35 pounds) exist within 1,000 miles of Georgia. A wolf/coyote misidentification is understandable but wolves are much taller and weigh over 100 pounds and coyotes max out at 40 pounds. They have a similar grizzled gray, brown and white coloration with pointed ears, long bushy tail and long straight legs. The panther miss-identification riddle is much less clear cut, especially if the panther report indicates a "black panther". There is no black color phase of panthers anywhere in the entire United States, and there never has been! The closest thing to it is a rare black color phase of the South American jaguar. There are a few in Central America but none in this country except in zoos.

Most are reported seen at night or at least in poor light, and most reports involve far away fleeting glimpses of running animals. There never seemed to be any evidence left behind: no tracks, no droppings, no hair, nothing. Wherever there was a track reported, it always turned out to be a dog track. Two panther sightings in broad daylight at close range were reported by professional foresters 20 years apart in Rabun County, not far from the South Carolina state line. In one case, the panther was observed stalking a deer! One 10-second video was submitted to DNR sometime in the late 1990s supposedly from Hart County, also on the South Carolina state line. All of these were tan/tawny color. None of these three big cats ever turned up again anywhere, dead or alive. Why is proximity to South Carolina potentially important? There are panthers in captivity in South Carolina that the SCDNR does not have records of, or have regulatory authority over. Some or all of the three incidents above could possibly have been escapees from somebody's confinement.

Another incident occurred about the same time as the above video. An escaped zoo cougar was killed in the Cohutta Wilderness near the Tennessee state line. Anonymous photos were circulating as "proof" of a wild cougar kill and finally showed up in a hunting magazine. The real story was soon revealed, but not before a rash of cougar sightings was reported in that general area. There was only one real zoo cougar and he was already dead. The power of suggestion is incredible!

Sometime in the early 2000s, we got reports of a black panther that was killed in the Georgia mountains and placed in a taxidermist's freezer in preparation for mounting. Information was sketchy, and it took awhile but one of the DNR conservation officers finally obtained the carcass and brought it to the Gainesville office for verification. We got our cameras out, loaded our film and got ready for the big event. Here came the officer with the frozen critter. Out of the black plastic bag came a frozen-stiff black house cat with a fierce snarl permanently frozen on his face! He sure looked mean with all those long, sharp pearly white teeth and yellow eyes but needed to gain at least 100 pounds to qualify as a real black panther! He was a big house cat but no bigger than 15 pounds. To this day, I wonder if that cat was ever mounted or not and if they still call it a black panther.

A Dog-Eat-Dog
World

Okay, I slipped a chapter into this book not directly related to wildlife, but I could not resist. It is my favorite true woodland story, and it goes like this.

Got dogs? My wife and I do, as do many of the wildlife watchers and outdoor enthusiasts who will read this book. We have a true and entertaining dog story for you.

Once upon a time years ago, we had a male golden retriever, Zack–a really laid-back and nice dog. Zack was a yard dog, allowed to roam free because he could handle his freedom without major problems, and our house and 36 acres is tucked a long way back from the highway. Occasionally, he would stroll about 400 yards down to our pond for a swim and come home wet, cool and refreshed. This arrangement was a peaceful co-existence for everyone… for a while.

I had always wanted a yellow lab – what better time to get a puppy! We wanted him and our two-year-old daughter to grow up together! If you have ever seen a six-week-old yellow lab puppy in person, there is no walking away with your hands in your pockets. We brought him home and named him Gentle Ben. At first he stayed mostly inside; then gradually was left outside with Zack–after all, it was summer and the weather was great. The puppy loved to play with (harass) Zack, climb all over him and bite him everywhere with his needle sharp teeth. Zack was tolerant, but once in a while would issue a warning growl when Ben bit too hard. They were inseparable; everywhere Zack went Ben tagged along. One day we came home from work and they were nowhere to be found, not even at the pond. At about dark, Zack showed up alone without Ben. He was wet and hungry and looked kind of relieved and peaceful.

We live in a sparsely populated rural area. By the next day, my wife and I split the neighborhood in half, each going door to door with pictures of the puppy. After several days, we were getting very discouraged. We knew our chances of finding Ben were slim.

It was two weeks later when we drove into the front yard and heard high-pitched yips from Zack's pen. We ran to the pen door and there was Ben, paws on the door, wagging his tail, but skinny as a rail! Someone had brought him home and put him in the pen. We wanted to thank the person but had no clue who it was.

Fast forward nine years later. Zack was almost 15. He was stone deaf and had only one eye. Hip problems had been creeping up on him for years as they do on lots of retrievers. For a couple of weeks, we would have to lift him up from a sitting to standing position, and he would take it from there for the rest of the day. One day Zack could not get up on his back legs even with us helping him. We had him put to sleep and could not help but cry.

Meanwhile, my friend had a four-year-old female yellow lab in heat. He knew Ben and wanted him to breed his dog. All went as planned, and about two months later she had a litter of seven beautiful pups.

At six weeks of age, we picked up our pup. By the next day his name was Ben Junior, Jay or sometimes J.J. for short. He was so cute and fuzzy and cuddly for everyone… except Ben. Now 10 years old, Ben tried to ignore the pup, even though he was his son. Meanwhile, Jay loved Ben; he looked just like a bigger yellow version of his mom! They were inseparable and we left them outside together. As Jay reached nine weeks, he was climbing all over Ben, biting, taunting, pulling, shaking various parts of Ben including ears, lips, skin, tail, feet and whatever he could grasp. Occasionally, Ben would yip in pain and sometimes let out a warning growl, but overall he appeared very tolerant and took it in stride. But, little did we know, Ben had a plan (borrowed from Zack).

We came home one day and they were gone. Ben returned at dark relieved and unconcerned, but no Jay. The next day, a neighbor called and said someone had pulled up in his driveway, dropped off Jay and sped away. We brought him home and put him with Ben, confident that the whole thing was a fluke. A few days later, it happened again. Ben showed up late in the evening without Jay. I went out in the yard and began calling Jay and heard a distant high-pitched yipping. I could barely see Jay barking behind the metal gate of a barn. He finally figured out his own way to get out. Jay ran up in the yard and proceeded to playfully bite Ben's ears, mouth and shoulders. Ben had that "Oh no, foiled again" look in his eyes.

We got a new name tag for Jay and it paid off immediately. Same deal, Ben came home by himself kind of peaceful looking. Just as we were getting ready to search, a neighbor called and said she had captured Jay as he was playing with her dog.

Why it took us so long to catch on to Ben's ploy, I really don't know, but the next few attempts by Ben to find a new home for the pup resulted in four failures (a failure was when Ben could not slip away from the pup before someone called us and we arrived). One place where Ben particularly wanted Jay to stay was with neighbors who had a big black lab just like Ben…only wrong color. Ben tried to leave Jay three times at this place, but these folks invariably called quickly, not giving Ben the chance to slip away.

The final straw and the last time we left the dogs together unsupervised for more than 10 seconds, we had our real revelation. Same scenario: we come home and the dogs are gone. This time there was a message on our recorder from a family one-half mile away. A phone call verified that our vagabond dogs had taken up at their house with a pool, a female rat terrier, and two young girls who loved dogs. We rushed down there for the rescue (the dogs did not think "rescue," they were having fun).

After thanking the dad several times, he told us how he remembered my wife coming by their home a few years ago with a yellow puppy picture of Ben and how over a week later, they found the skinny pup huddled underneath an old car in their backyard. He said, "Yeah, I loaded the pup, brought him to your house and put him in your pen."

My eyes now as big as saucers, I pointed to Ben (who looked kind of sheepish) and said, "That's him! That's the pup you brought home to us nine years ago!"

He shook his head in disbelief. We finally thanked him, long overdue for the deed!

Well, I can put two and two together just as well as anyone. Was this a coincidence or was this Ben's last-gasp attempt at finding a new home for the pup? It was by far the farthest away. Did he remember his own visit here nine years ago? What if Ben himself was lost again? All I can say is that it's a good thing for dog name tags, phones, good neighbors and little girls!

Operation extreme vigilance was now in effect at our house. Those dogs were never again left together outside of the pen unless I was with them.

Fast forward again. Ben had recently died of cancer at 16½ years old (we have his ashes in an urn), and Jay was now five years old…our only dog. He couldn't be left alone for more than 10 seconds or he would make a beeline off our hill, visit several neighborhood dogs and finally end up in a new neighbor's yard with their little dog over a mile away.

This happened at least five times and he never came home from there. Soon he shifted to another neighbor even farther away who had three dogs. He played with his buddies, then curled up and slept in their front yard just like he owned the place! We had to go get him every time.

Lonely for canine company, I guess it was time for us to get a new pup, so here we went again!

Fast forward one last time. We got a dachshund puppy and named him Chili. At seven weeks old, he weighed a whopping three pounds! He immediately took up with Jay, now 10 years old and 100 pounds. When Jay was catching a nap, Chili would climb up on his back, curl up and go to sleep. Chili's favorite activity was to bite around Jay's mouth, ears, legs and tail. Jay was a gentle giant and was very tolerant of all this, even though I am sure those needle sharp teeth hurt him. Jay's only reaction was to get up, turn in circles avoiding those little jaws and issue warning barks one at a time "Woof…Woof…Woof!"

I think you know what happened next. It happened when Chili was about five months old. Somehow, Jay pulled up his screw-down 25 foot cable and bailed off the top of our hill in the same direction that he always went, followed closely by Chili. We were home when it happened but did not notice for several minutes. As soon as I did, I took off after them in our truck, trying to cut them off at the pass! Across the highway, down the dirt road, across the creek I went, looking in everyone's yards. It was a heavily wooded area, and seeing them in a yard or on the road would be a stroke of luck. No luck. I came home, got my wife and some water, and we were just going out the door for round two when the phone rang. It was one of our neighbors about a half mile away who had called in Jay's barely legible rabies tag number and got our name and number from the vet's office (a personal friend of ours). He was holding Jay by his 25-foot cable and keeping him happy. We got directions and got in the truck. Ironically, I had been by that same house in round one of the search before Jay had arrived there. We were there in five minutes, unhooked Jay from his cable, dropped the tailgate and he loaded up. Handshakes and many thanks were in order! But where was Chili? He was not with Jay, and the neighbor had not seen him.

We got back in our truck to look for him. It would be dark shortly, and coyotes would soon be on the prowl. Chili is no match for a coyote! We had not driven more than 100 yards, crossed the creek and up the hill when we saw Chili running down the middle of the road toward us with a car behind him. We stopped got out and waved our arms to alert the driver who had already seen our little dog and slowed down. My wife ran up to Chili and picked him up. He was so happy to see us, his tail going 100 mph! We thanked the lady driver, turned around and drove home. I said to my wife, "Do you realize just how lucky we are?" Jay was headed for his favorite house with the three dogs whether Chili was with him or not. If he had made it with Chili in tow, he would have played awhile, dropped Chili off and snuck back home without him. He knew the drill, even though it had been a long time since he was the victim! If Chili was not with him, I am afraid that Chili's fate was to have been attacked and killed by a coyote.

Does the story end here? It does, because Jay recently lost his battle with cancer. Up until the very end, he never lost his appetite or stopped wagging his tail. He was 10 and a half years old. About nine months later, Chili was attacked and killed by coyotes on our own property.

Note: This chapter is dedicated to Zack, Ben, Jay, and Chili.

WOODLAND TERRORISTS

F ree-ranging dogs, including some that are family pets, can cause significant problems with white-tailed deer, wild turkeys and many other wildlife species. Problems begin with harassment but can often include actual killing of several species of wildlife especially deer fawns and wild turkeys. First of all, free-ranging dogs in most cases are not always so-called wild dogs. In many cases, they are family pets who have been allowed to roam free because it's "too cruel" to keep them confined or in a pen. On my own property a few years ago, I witnessed a neighbor's Rottweiler chase down a flock of wild turkeys and catch one of the hens. That hen and others in the flock had difficulty getting airborne fast enough to escape the dog because of an earlier drenching rain which had left their flight feathers wet and heavy.

In an Alabama study done a few years ago, dogs were identified as the second most common nest predator of wild turkeys, following closely behind raccoons. In some cases, they were able to catch and kill the nesting hen turkey as well as destroy the eggs. In other cases, pure harassment of the hen turkey by dogs will cause it to abandon its nest for good, never returning. In the same study, dogs ranked as the number one predator of turkey poults. Of 400 young turkey poults, 279 died during the study. Cause of death was established for 136 of these (the rest were unknown). Predators were responsible for 111 deaths (82 percent of total known deaths). Dogs caught 32 (29 percent), raccoons 14 (13 percent), bobcats and gray foxes 11 (10 percent), hawks and owls took 22 (20 percent). There should be no excuse for the domestic dog, man's best friend, to inflict such a significant loss on our valuable wildlife such as wild turkeys. It is virtually 100 percent preventable, just by using a simple common sense approach to dog confinement.

In another study done in the mountains of North Carolina, dogs were used to conduct experimental chases of radio-collared white-tailed deer. Of 20 experimental chases, two deer were captured and killed by the packs of dogs. Rugged, rocky mountainous terrain caused some deer to be injured by breaking a leg during the chase and these were subsequently caught by the dogs. Captured deer were sent to the Southeastern Cooperative Wildlife Disease Study for analysis, where it was discovered they also had high parasite loads of lungworms and were in a weakened condition with low fat levels in late-winter and early spring. Bottom line: dogs in packs regularly pursue and harass adult deer and occasionally kill one, especially if the deer is injured or weakened by food shortages or parasites.

The extent of dog predation on newborn deer fawns is unknown but probably occurs quite frequently. In June, July and August, when fawns are common in the woods, chance encounters with a dog can often be fatal, especially if the fawn is less than one month old and cannot out-run the dogs.

The list of potential dog-wildlife problems is long and includes the harassing or killing of groundhogs, raccoons, opossums, skunks, rabbits, squirrels, quail, grouse and other ground-nesting birds. Much of the bad stuff that coyotes are accused of, such as killing sheep, goats or calves, is actually caused by free-ranging dogs. As part of my job as a wildlife biologist, I investigated several of these after being contacted by farmers or landowners who said coyotes had killed their animals. Based on the sign at the kill scene (hair, tracks or scat), I would estimate that over 75 percent of the kills were made by dogs, not coyotes or other predators.

Ironically, the roaming family pet appears to be a more efficient predator than the wild dog because the family pet is well fed and healthy and hunts more for fun than for food. They are likely faster, bigger and stronger than their wild counterparts. Their predatory instinct is just as strong as that of the wild dog.

A study done by a wildlife professor and his students at Auburn University focused on radio tracking his own two Brittany Spaniels. The results were eye-opening! The dogs slept on his porch or in his yard almost all day long. At night under cover of darkness they terrorized wildlife ranging from rabbits to deer almost all night long, returning to the porch before daylight to rest up for the next night of "fun"! This dog owner (the professor) would never have guessed the nightly harassment was taking place had he not put radio collars on both of his dogs and found out for himself.

There is one more very important factor for dog owners to consider. Free-ranging dogs are at great risk for their own health and survival! They are subject to greatly increased contact with wild animals carrying diseases such as rabies, distemper, parvovirus or leptospirosis. Risk of heartworms also skyrockets because of exposure to millions of mosquitoes which are very active at night. They are at great risk of being killed by cars and many are permanently lost or picked up by dog thieves. They can also be caught in a fence or tumble into an open well without a chance of being rescued.

The forest is no place for free-ranging dogs, it is the home of valuable native wildlife populations that can suffer from harassment or death. Dogs and wildlife don't mix. If you value your dog and also value wildlife, be a responsible pet owner and keep your dogs confined!

CAT INVADERS

H ave you asked your cat what he had for a midnight snack last night? If he could talk, he would probably say a mouse, a rabbit, or a flying squirrel. These are all creatures that are active at night and high on a cat's list of favorites. What about breakfast? It probably included a goldfinch, song sparrow, wood thrush or bobwhite quail, which are active during daylight hours and spend lots of time feeding or nesting on the ground. On the average, song birds make up over 20 percent of the diets of domestic cats. This is truly a nationwide problem. Observations of free-ranging domestic cats show that some individuals can kill over 1,000 wild animals per year! These are not only birds and mammals but also reptiles, amphibians, fish and even insects. Free-ranging cats living in small towns kill an average of 14 wild animals per year, but rural cats kill many more than urban or suburban cats. Studies have shown that 90 percent of rural cats' diets are wild animals, and less than 10 percent killed no wild animals.

Nationwide, 64 million domestic cats and tens of millions of stray cats kill an estimated one billion birds in the U.S. annually. Cats have been responsible for the extinction of more bird species (33) than from any other cause except habitat destruction. In some parts of rural Georgia, densities of free-ranging cats can reach 114 cats per square mile! This number is many times more abundant than all mid-sized native predators (such as foxes, raccoons, and skunks) combined.

Although cats make affectionate pets, many hunt as effectively as wild predators. However, they have three big advantages over wild predators. First, people protect domestic cats from disease, predators, and competition–all factors that control numbers of wild predators. Second, they often have a very dependable supply of cat food at home. Third, cat densities are not limited by territoriality among the male tom cats. However, there is a new serious predator out there now who is putting quite a dent in feral cat population numbers, and that is coyotes. It is kind of ironic, but these canines are also non-native predators who have invaded the forest ecosystem of all the central and eastern states. In Georgia, they were illegally stocked by fox hunters and also got here on their own moving from west to east through Alabama and Tennessee.

In summary, free-ranging cats are abundant and widespread predators which can exist at much higher densities than native predators. They kill large numbers of wildlife, especially birds. They compete with native predators, and they can harbor a variety of diseases including distemper, toxoplasmosis, and even rabies. What can you do to help? Keep only as many pet cats as you can feed and care for. Well-fed, neutered females stay closest to farm buildings and do most of their killing where rodent control is needed the most. Neuter your cats to prevent them from breeding, and encourage other pet owners to do so. If at all possible, for the sake of your cat's safety and local wildlife, keep your cat indoors. Outdoor cats only have an average lifespan of two to five years, while indoor cats can live up to 17 years! Locate bird feeders in sites with no cover for cats to ambush birds. Do not dispose of unwanted cats by releasing them in rural areas but bring them to the local animal shelter. Eliminate sources of food that might attract stray cats. Do not under any circumstances feed stray cats! This benefits no one, the cats suffer from diseases, native wildlife suffers, and stray cat colonies are a serious source of disease for animals and humans.

Folks concerned with the welfare of animals can improve the lives of their cats and the many native wildlife species that suffer from cat predation and cat competition with native predators by practicing these common sense guidelines for dealing with domestic and stray cats. Remember those one billion songbirds. Do not let your cats be terrorists or dinner for coyotes!

Chunks of Skunks and Other Stuff on the Roads

O ver 35 years as a wildlife biologist living and working in north Georgia, I learned a few things about wildlife, their life cycles and their movements. Sometimes I did not even have to set foot in the woods to figure out what was happening there. In mid to late winter, I could tell by riding down the highway, even with my eyes closed. Guess what? It is striped skunk breeding season! Those noxious, smelly, black and white, flat, furry spots all over the roads do not lie. Skunks move more during breeding season, they cross more roads and they get run over far more often. How is that for putting two and two together!

The female skunk survivors, after a 62- to 68-day gestation period, give birth to somewhere between two to 10 kits in April to May. Adults weigh 6-14 pounds and are roughly house-cat size.

A skunks' diet is varied and includes insects, small mammals, worms, snails, grains, nuts, fruits, reptiles, vegetation, amphibians, birds, eggs, carrion and garbage. See why we have such high skunk populations right now due to high reproduction and plenty of skunk food available? The high population picture is also due to numerous chicken houses supplying skunk food in the form of both dead chickens and rats. All this contributes to a high incidence of rabies in north Georgia recently. Skunks and raccoons are the two most common carriers of rabies, and both populations are high right now. By the way, it is also raccoon breeding season from February and into March; you can tell that by flat, furry, ring- tailed spots on roads too. Numbers of both of these animals used to be controlled by hunting and/or trapping, but now for the most part, these are long lost activities in such a civilized world where animal furs are worthless. Instead their populations are now controlled by diseases including rabies, distemper, parvovirus, tularemia, leptospirosis and others.

If confronted by a live skunk, do not panic. Skunks are mild-tempered and will not generally defend themselves by spraying unless they are provoked. When agitated, they can spray accurately up to 10 feet or more. Before spraying, they will stomp their front feet rapidly and arch their tail up over their back as a warning. If you see this, make a slow, quiet retreat. A skunks' spray is usually directed toward the eyes and may temporarily cause blindness and nausea. The spray is a hard-to-remove, horrible-smelling, oily liquid produced by glands under its large bushy tail. A veterinarian friend of mine recommends an easy home remedy for removing skunk odors from people or pets. Mix one bottle of hydrogen peroxide with one box of baking soda and add a few drops of dish- washing liquid. Start scrubbing!

Meanwhile, the incidence of nest destruction of ground-nesting birds such as quail, wild turkeys and several songbirds by skunks, raccoons and opossums has greatly increased. These nest predators either run the hen off her nest or kill her and gobble up all the eggs. Most of the time, they do more damage to turkey and quail nests than do coyotes. By the way, rabies in opossums is extremely rare; they are highly resistant to it.

Incidentally, it is opossum breeding season in late winter too as evidenced by all the flat, furry, bare-tailed spots on the roads. A good friend and classmate of mine did a possum radio-telemetry study for his master's degree at the University of Georgia back in the early 1970s and soon found out the leading cause of mortality in opossums was what he called the "B.F. Goodrich Syndrome." No kidding! I'm sure that conclusion still applies today. It is certainly a complex web of survival and death for these small furbearers/predators/scavengers, especially with many more highways and speeding vehicles thrown in the mix.

In March, skunk, opossum and raccoon road kills slow down, but deer and groundhog road-kill problems go up as spring green-up begins. Grasses alongside highways green-up first, and deer and groundhogs begin feeding on them. Deer road kills spike in March every year. Deer movements, slowed in winter by cold weather, increase again during this green-up as they try to regain lost body weight by eating new plant growth full of protein. Next to the November rutting season, spring green-up is the number two road-kill season for deer. Annual estimates peg deer road- kills at 30,000 to 50,000 a year in Georgia alone!

Deer populations are controlled by hunters, not vehicles or diseases, thank goodness! Annual deer harvests in Georgia average around 300,000 to 350,000 per year, 10 times higher than deer road kills. Regulated hunting is the only way to control deer populations on a large scale. Other methods including road kills are a disaster. If we ever let deer populations get out of control like those of skunks, raccoons and opossums, we are all sunk and so are the animals, whether they die a slow painful death from diseases or a quick violent death from a vehicle. Meanwhile, we all face occasional danger from hitting a deer on the highway, being subject to disgusting odors emanating from chunks of skunks, or encountering a rabid animal. Be careful out there!

SCARED OF SNAKES

Are you scared of or worried about snakes? You probably shouldn't be, because most snakes are harmless to you and actually perform a valuable service to us by eating rodents, insects and even other snakes. Most snakes, when given the opportunity, will quickly leave the area and run for cover to avoid people. Coiling and striking are usually defensive maneuvers reserved for last resort. What you can do to avoid encounters with snakes is keep your eyes open and watch where you step. Snakes both venomous and non-venomous can become very aggressive when stepped on and strike in self-defense. Even common black rat snakes can be aggressive if you aggravate them. Their bite is painful, but they are not venomous.

Snakes are especially active in August and September, so encounters with them are more likely at this time. September temperatures are mostly ideal for snakes, and they are also looking for a last meal or two before finding a place to den for the winter. Populations are also at their highest during this time because of reproduction which occurred since spring.

If you don't want snakes around your yard, remove cover such as rock piles, wood piles, debris, thickets and other places for snakes to hide. If you have lots of mice, then you will automatically have lots of snakes because mice are a big part of most snake diets. Snake repellents are not effective outdoors but may be somewhat effective if snakes are getting into basements, carports, outbuildings or crawl spaces. Lime sulfur applied as a spray on rags, or moth balls, placed in snake resting areas under buildings may help repel them.

How do you know if the snake in front of you is venomous? There are only three species of venomous snakes in north Georgia. These are the timber (or canebreak) rattlesnake, copperhead, and pigmy rattlesnake. Most of the rest of the states north and northeast of Georgia only have two species, the copperhead and timber rattler. States to the east, south and west add back the pigmy plus the cottonmouth to the list. On the coastal plain from Mississippi to North Carolina, the eastern diamondback and coral snake also occur. See below.

The timber rattler is a stout snake that is usually brown with black crossbands in the shape of chevrons. The pigmy rattler has dark round or oval blotches with the central line being the most distinct. Two rows of less distinct blotches appear on the sides. All species of rattlesnakes have rattles on the ends of their tails and most of the time they will warn you by rattling before they strike. The rattle is unmistakable and sounds a lot like a baby's rattle. Other than in the mountains, both species of rattlesnakes are becoming uncommon or even rare in North

Georgia as their habitat and cover disappears as a result of development.

The copperhead, our most common venomous snake, is stout with tan or light brown skin and dark brown or reddish hourglass-shaped crossbands that are narrowest at the midline of the back. These bands widen as they go down the side of the snake. It gets its name from the coppery color on top of its head. The illustration on the first page of this chapter is a copperhead. Copperheads (also called highland moccasin) thrive in overgrown, brushy areas and old homesites. All venomous snakes have triangular-shaped heads, vertical elliptical eye pupils (like cats), and a pit between the nose and eye. If you're close enough to observe these characteristics, you are probably too close if the snake is still alive!

Surprise, surprise, there are no cottonmouths, diamondback rattlesnakes or so-called venomous water moccasins in north Georgia (except for a small population of cottonmouths on the Etowah River near Rome). There are no venomous water snakes in lakes Hartwell, Lanier, Burton, Chatuge, Nottely, Carter's, Blue Ridge or Allatoona.

Normally, venomous snakes are not aggressive and are somewhat sluggish. Unless stepped on, picked up, or seriously aggravated, they usually won't strike. An exception is when they are shedding their skin, which they do about twice each summer. When shedding is in progress, the layer of skin over their eyes turns cloudy and they cannot see very well, making them more prone to strike.

You do have friends in the snake world! The eastern king snake, which is shiny black with a prominent white chain link pattern on its back, will readily kill and eat any of the venomous snakes that are smaller than itself. The black rat snake, probably the most common snake in most of the eastern half of the country, is jet black with white specks on his back with a white belly. They are one of nature's best rodent predators, competing with the venomous snakes for the same food supply and doing a good job of it because of their greater numbers. Do not kill these snakes or any other non-venomous snakes; it is illegal in Georgia and most other states. They are an important part of our environment. Even venomous snakes have their place and should not be harmed except when found in close proximity to homes or towns.

Back in the early 1970s, I was a counselor at a summer camp on a National Wildlife Refuge. We had about 50 big city teenage kids working out in the woods on various projects and staying overnight in tents. One day one of the boys caught a copperhead, and another captured a king snake. They were both about three to three and a half feet long. We had a cage at the camp and put both snakes in together to see what would happen. It did not take long for the king snake to wrap up in coils around the copperhead and constrict it to death. He maneuvered around to put his mouth around the venomous snake's head and started swallowing inch by inch. He swallowed about half the snake that evening before bedtime. By the next morning, only an inch of the copperhead's tail was sticking out of the king snake's mouth! None of us had ever seen that before, and I bet we all remember that vividly to this day!

Once, I unknowingly stepped within two inches of the head of a coiled copperhead and he did not strike, though he could have easily bitten me on the ankle. On another occasion, a copperhead ran between my legs fleeing as I stood there with a garden sprayer spraying weed killer.

My closest encounter with a timber rattler came upon returning home to find my golden retriever circling a big five-foot coiled rattler in my driveway just 30 feet from my front door! He was rattling his tail like crazy. Somehow, the dog had sense enough to keep out of striking distance while he was going round and round the snake. I got my .22 rifle, got the dog away, and shot the snake. I could not help but think of how many times my wife, daughter and I had walked all over and around our yard even in the dark!

Some strikes from venomous snakes do not inject venom through the fangs and therefore can be relatively harmless. When venom is injected, the pain is worse than a bee sting, and there will be two fang puncture marks. If you have been bitten by a non-venomous snake, you will see a U-shaped row of puncture marks but not two fang marks. If you suspect the snake is venomous, kill the snake and bring it with you to the emergency room for positive identification. Don't panic, keep calm, and don't run or raise your pulse rate. Nearly all snakebite victims recover completely in a short time with proper medical care.

In summary, don't let an overactive fear of snakes keep you from conducting your normal outdoor activities. Venomous snakes are usually not aggressive, they do not exist in large numbers, and your chances of encountering one are slim. Just be alert, use your eyes and watch your step! A detailed web guide to Georgia and South Carolina snakes is available from the University of Georgia at: www.uga.edu/srelherp/snakes /index.htm.

TO BATTLE BEAVERS
OR NOT

After being virtually eliminated from the eastern half of our country in the early part of this century by fur trappers, beavers have made an incredible comeback. They currently inhabit virtually every river system in Georgia and most all of the other eastern states including all of the big lakes. By traveling upstream from lakes in rivers, creeks and branches, they have easy access to all streams, ponds, wetlands or any source of water. This can be good news or bad news. On the good side, beaver ponds provide excellent wildlife habitat, hunting and fishing opportunities and wetland habitat for dozens of plants and animals, especially fish, waterfowl, wading birds and numerous amphibians. Beaver ponds are among the most diverse wildlife habitats in the country. They are also useful for irrigation, flood control and maintaining water tables during droughts. Most importantly, they catch silt from storm runoff and prevent it from moving farther downstream into farm ponds, rivers or lakes.

I have two beaver dams on streams feeding the upper end of my pond, and both help catch muddy storm runoff from my neighbor's steep pasture (that is assuming we get an ample supply of rain and pull out of some of the most recent droughts). They also provide wood duck brood-rearing habitat for the tiny ducklings that hatch out of my three wood duck boxes. They provide a valuable service for me if they can keep themselves out of trouble. Do not get me wrong, I like beavers–most of the time!

Now the bad news: they can cross the line from hero to villain pretty easily and do so by girdling or cutting down my favorite trees. One year they cut down 12 of my best apple trees in only two or three nights before I even realized it! They came out of the water and waddled past some tender, less valuable trees such as poplar, willow and sweetgum to get my apples 30 yards up the hill from the pond. One year they munched the tops out of all the beans in my garden, and another time they got into my corn, cut the stalks and drug them into the pond, ripe ears and all!

What about ugly? Another year they girdled three huge white oak trees which of course caused them to die gradually and stand there like a skeleton until a storm blew them over into the pond. A few years ago, they girdled my all-time favorite tree - a beech tree that had to be a least 150 years old! Now it has died and fallen. Each incident stimulated retaliation on my part. I would get my rifle and sit quietly waiting for them to come out just before dark. Each year, I shot one or two to slow things down and ease the continuous damage, knowing that there always seemed to be two or three left in the pond to survive and proliferate. These were the ones who learned not to come out of their underwater holes in the pond bank until after dark. Still, damage slowed down greatly after these shootings.

I also got to work and protected my most valuable remaining trees with a skirt of 36-inch 2x4 welded wire fastened loosely around the tree trunk to allow for future tree growth. This kept the remaining beavers and any new ones from cutting them down or damaging them. I put a 24-inch chicken wire fence between the pond and garden to keep them out of the beans and corn. The fence was 100 feet long, and they never figured out how to skirt around it on the ends.

Other techniques to repel beavers include commercial repellents such as Hinder (smells like ammonia) or Ropel (extremely bitter) that can be sprayed or brushed on the tree trunks of valuable trees. These work well but probably need to be re-applied every two to four weeks depending on the frequency of rainfall.

Probably the most effective beaver control is trapping. There is no economical or effective live trap for beavers, they just don't like to go in them except on rare occasions. Conibear traps (snap jaw kill traps) are by far the most effective traps for beavers. A good trapper can pretty much wipe out a colony of beavers (usually four to six) in a farm pond or beaver pond without endangering other non-target animals because the traps are set mostly underwater. Obviously, beaver control on rivers or lakes is more difficult because of extensive connected habitat and wider beaver movements. Effective trapping usually requires experience that you and I don't have. If you are serious about beaver control, get an expert. The state DNR in Georgia and many other states maintain a list of nuisance beaver trappers who really know how to catch the critters. Of course, trappers will charge a fee to come out and trap beavers depending on the extent of their expenses incurred. Traps must be checked every day.

Beaver pelt prices have been low for many years, and trappers cannot even come close to covering their expenses by selling pelts. After a "trap out" it usually takes one to five years for new beavers to move back into a farm pond. It is much more of a gamble concerning re-colonization time in the big lakes and rivers. Georgia DNR also has a free brochure called *"Controlling Beaver Damage in Georgia"* available at all district offices. The brochure goes into much more detail than this chapter. The internet is loaded with good information on beaver control.

To recap, under most conditions, shooting is usually the cheapest and easiest control method for beavers. It's legal all year long in Georgia (check the regulations in your state) and most effective at dusk. Be very careful as some bullets can ricochet off the surface of the water and end up on dry land down range! Trapping can be very effective if done by an expert and will usually remove more beavers than shooting. Be prepared to pay.

Finally, beavers tend to repopulate an area repeatedly. In preparation for this, protect your valuable trees, shrubs and gardens with fencing or repellents. Low populations of beavers can be quite beneficial by catching muddy water runoff behind their dams. By the way, contrary to popular belief they are strict vegetarians and do not eat fish! They won't hurt the fishing at all in your farm pond or anywhere else.

QUAIL IN TROUBLE

I f you ask anyone in Georgia or throughout the East and Midwest what has happened to bobwhite quail, almost unanimously they will quickly answer "too many predators" and rattle off species like hawks, coyotes, free-ranging house cats or any number of predatory culprits, including nest predators such as raccoons, possums and skunks. Ok, guilty on all counts to some degree, but these are not the main culprits.

Have you heard any bobwhite quail whistling lately around your backyard, farm or hunting property? When was the last time you saw any? If you have, consider yourself lucky, because these sights and sounds are getting pretty rare lately.

When I first came to Georgia in 1972 to attend the University of Georgia, quail were almost everywhere. I rented a house trailer in Madison County near Hull, Georgia. If I could get home from classes by mid-afternoon and find my landlord, we would load up his bird dog (half pointer, half setter which was known in those days as a "drop") and go quail hunting. He knew every farmer in the county and had permission to hunt around every soybean field. At that time the county was virtually wall-to-wall soybean fields. By sunset, we would have flushed from three to nine coveys of quail by methodically moving from one soybean field to the next, not even bothering to hunt single birds after the covey rise. He would occasionally get a limit (12 birds) and I would occasionally get three or four on a good day. These were my first-ever attempts at hunting quail, and the birds were mostly too fast for me!

Here we are over 40 years later. What in the world happened? Those small soybean or corn fields with heavy cover around the edges, weedy creek drains, and weeds in the corners have turned into pasture, hayfields, pine trees, and subdivisions! While deer and turkey can get by and make a pretty good living under these conditions, quail cannot. Incidentally, high deer populations which occurred in Georgia and all over the eastern half of the country in the 1980s and 1990s reduced or even eliminated lots of wild legumes, which are vitally important quail plants. These included partridge pea, lespedezas and many other seed-bearing species important to quail especially in winter.

Quail need food and cover in small connected patches. They need plenty of seed to eat, especially in fall and winter. They need plenty of nesting and brood-rearing cover which is found in fallow fields, cropland borders, hedgerows, and blackberry or plum thickets. People used to burn their pine woods once every two or three years. When is the last time you saw anyone doing that? Late-winter burning resulted in good food and cover areas for quail, especially adjacent to cropland or old fields.

Fescue and Bermudagrass make great pasture and hayfields but terrible quail habitat. Quail can hardly walk through these aggressive, perennial turf grasses, never mind find any food or overhead cover. They don't eat fescue seed or Bermudagrass seed, nor do these sod grasses produce very many insects for quail chicks to feed on when they are just a little bigger than your thumb.

The old timers (I hope I'm not one of those yet) blame the quail decline on hawks and other predators. While there are certainly plenty of predators around, both furry and feathery, there are also many examples in parts of south Georgia and other states where predator populations are even higher than here and quail populations are still good due to intensive management efforts. If you have good quail habitat, you can have quail despite a wide array of predators!

What can we do now to get quail back? The answer is not cheap or easy. We cannot go back to the old days of corn and soybeans. There are various state programs around the Southeast aimed at encouraging or even funding quail management. Ours is called the Bobwhite Quail Initiative funded by the sale of special vehicle license plates. However, it is confined to a 15-county area in south Georgia where there is still is a lot of row-crop agriculture. The program used to pay farmers incentives for certain quail management practices but was discontinued in 2011 due to lack of funding. Even though the program is not available for north Georgia or many other places further north where there may not be enough row crop agriculture, folks serious about quail could establish similar management practices such as establishing hedgerows, field borders, and controlled burning on their own farmlands or forests.

In addition, there are a lot of bare, clean fencerows that could easily be allowed to grow up in plum trees, briars, honeysuckle and all kinds of wild plants beneficial to quail. Certain plantings work very well, including bicolor lespedeza, browntop millet, Egyptian wheat, grain sorghum, winter wheat, and partridge pea. Even strips disked in the fall and left fallow produce an abundant ragweed crop the following spring for nesting and brood-rearing cover.

Unfortunately, there may still be a much bigger landscape problem when these small but quality habitats are distant from the next good quail habitat. Sometimes these gaps stretch for miles. How are quail going to populate and reproduce on your quality habitat when the nearest quail are over a mile away with no habitat connection? They just do not move that far.

Don't fall into the trap of buying and stocking pen-raised birds to boost the quail population! Most won't survive for a week, and it is extremely rare for any to survive and reproduce from one year to the next! It's been tried and failed thousands of times all over the country. Think about it: if conditions were right, there would be more wild quail there already. Trying to raise quail populations by stocking pen-raised birds is like pouring water into a bucket with holes in it. You can, however, release pen-raised quail on your own property to train bird dogs. Make sure this practice is legal in your state. Some enthusiasts even have elaborate systems of holding quail for several months for dog-training purposes. For more information, go to: http://www.qualitywildlife.com.

Wild quail management is a habitat issue and certainly a difficult one in Georgia and many other eastern states. If you build it, they may or may not come. However, it may be worth a try if your property is positioned well in relation to an already existing quail population. If you need more advice on how to build it, contact a wildlife biologist with your state wildlife agency.

CANADA GEESE:
SPECTACLE OR PEST

There is no greater wild spectacle than the sight and sound of a large V formation of geese passing high overhead and honking back and forth to each other. On the flip side, there is nothing more frustrating than a large flock feeding on your manicured lawn and leaving their mess of droppings and feathers. Here is our local story along with some advice.

From 1978 through 1982, a total of over 2,000 geese from Tennessee, New York, and Pennsylvania were caught, trucked south and stocked all over northeast Georgia. These geese formed the nucleus of today's thriving non-migratory flock. The same thing was happening in virtually all the other eastern states whether by stocking or natural re-population. In Georgia, there were basically two goals: 1) to establish a viable resident population throughout a state where Canada geese had been extirpated and migratory Canada geese had been short stopped by northern states; 2) to establish a huntable surplus, where the goose population could be controlled by legal, carefully regulated hunting.

Needless to say, the geese have done well, expanding their numbers and range faster than anyone could have predicted. They nest in spring, laying two to seven large eggs which hatch after about 35 days of incubation. Chick survival is high, as geese are large, aggressive and loyal parents, making them successful reproducers. The chicks are virtually invulnerable to all predators after two weeks of age–except large dogs, coyotes and bobcats. Their numbers have exploded all over the country.

There has now been a limited hunting season for geese in Georgia since 1993. The carefully regulated hunts have been conservative so far but have helped control goose numbers from further increase. Actual declines in goose numbers have occurred in some problem areas such as parts of several of the big lakes, but there are still some troublesome spots. Trouble greatly intensifies in the early summer starting around the first of June, when the geese are flightless for about six weeks. They shed all 20 of their long flight feathers at the same time and re-grow new strong ones to coincide with the growth of their goslings' first set of flight feathers. Flight capability usually returns by early to mid-July.

Meanwhile, if you are having problems with geese, there are some solutions which you can implement. First and foremost, YOU MUST NOT FEED THE GEESE! Wild geese become tame very easily when they get a handout and can move in to stay for an extended time (kind of like the dreaded in-laws). If you are in this predicament already, one solution is a scare pistol loaded with bangers or screamers to frighten the birds away. These are available for sale from USDA Wildlife Services, Athens, GA

(1-8664USDAWS). This option is quite effective but does need to be repeated over a period of time. Since geese prefer to land on water and walk to short grass, another tactic which appears very promising is reflective flagging tape hung on a horizontal string fence between the edge of the water and the grazing area. Wide reflective mylar tape attached to the top of 3-foot stakes around the lawn or garden also works. Red helium balloons also work especially in big agricultural fields such as corn, soybeans or wheat.

For long term reduction of goose problems, landscape modification may be the best solution. The addition of shrubs and hedges as barriers between the water and feeding area keeps geese from walking onto the lawn and makes them feel insecure or nervous.

Obviously, if the situation warrants, especially on private farm ponds, get some goose hunters in there when the hunting season begins to harvest a few and scare the rest of the flock from using that area for a pretty good while. Goose breast is good table fare if prepared and cooked correctly. Cut it in thin slices, marinate it in soy sauce, lime juice and olive oil, and fry it no longer than three minutes per side. Do not over-cook it or you will convert it into shoe leather! To be very safe, make ground goose or goose jerky using any recipe meant for beef.

For golf courses, large parks, recreation areas and serious problems, there is a spray-on repellant available called Rejex-It. For information, go to: www.rejexit.com/MigrateTurfgeeserepellent.php or **for more information, call 1-866-53-BIRDS (1-866-532-4737).** Also, specially trained herding or goose-chasing dogs and handlers are available for a fee. The handler's goal is to train the geese to avoid the sensitive area by harassing the flock. How many repetitions does it take? I do not know, but I am sure it varies. Contact your state wildlife agency for assistance on the above two options, which are obviously appropriate for golf courses and parks where large flocks can congregate and consume the lush, short grass.

In the meantime, the geese are here to stay, and we all need to work together to figure out ways to tolerate and prevent some of the problems. There is nothing more symbolic of wildness or more pleasant to observe than a large V formation of geese overhead, honking back and forth to each other. Even the worst goose haters seem to enjoy the spectacle, as long as the geese don't land on their lawn or pasture!

WOOD DUCKS: CLASS OF AMERICAN WATERFOWL

T he wood duck is the most common duck found in most of the eastern states. It is also one of only two species of ducks that traditionally nest here (in addition to the hooded merganser) and is considered by many to be the most beautiful of all American waterfowl. Wood ducks were not always abundant. Thanks to state and federal protection, taxes on firearms and ammunition (the Pittman-Robertson Act) and an aggressive nesting-box program, wood ducks made an amazing recovery from the brink of extinction beginning in the 1930s. Most of the decline was caused by lack of natural nesting cavities, illegal harvest and over-harvest. Now they are abundant and protected by carefully controlled hunting seasons and bag limits in all of the states.

Once you have observed a wood duck's characteristic and distinctive colors and patterns, it is hard to mistake the "woody" for any other duck. The adult male has a sleek crest and its head displays a red bill, red eyes, green head, and striking white stripes on its face. It also has a large white throat patch and "fingerlike" extensions on its cheek and neck as well as iridescent dark green-blue back and wings. The female is less flashy (which is true of most female birds) with a gray bill, white teardrop-shaped patch around her eyes, white throat, and gray-brown head, neck and body. Their call is not even close to a quack but rather a high-pitched, squealing, two-note flight call emitted by the female. The male gives a soft up-slurred whistle while swimming.

About half the size of a mallard, the wood duck is a type of dabbling duck, meaning it forages on or near the water's surface for food as opposed to diving for food on the bottom. The diet of a wood duck includes hard mast (acorns), many species of seeds and soft mast (berries), insects (including beetles, bugs, ants and spiders), aquatic invertebrates (mollusks, snails, etc.), and aquatic plants. Like most birds, their diets vary depending on the time of year. During the fall and winter, acorns, other nuts and seeds are extremely important because they are high in fat, enabling woodies to migrate south or southwest and survive the harsher winter months. For the flight back to their nesting grounds, they continue eating remaining hard mast but also feed on more animal foods while preparing their bodies for early spring breeding and egg- laying.

Wood duck hens lay about one egg per day for two weeks. They incubate about 12 eggs for approximately 28 days and hatch the eggs in March and April on lakes, rivers, farm ponds and beaver swamps all over the East. Both nesting boxes on my pond are occupied pretty much every spring! Spring and summer food requirements shift toward finding higher protein foods like insects, some weed seeds and aquatic weedy vegetation to promote growth of young ducklings.

Because of their dependence on both acorns and tree cavities for nesting, wood ducks are closely associated with the forested wetland habitats throughout their range. Woodies seldom venture far from oak woodlands and associated wetlands which they use for feeding, resting and nesting. Their distribution is essentially confined to riparian corridors and other areas of lowland forest interspersed with freshwater ponds, lakes, marshes, and swamps. Beaver ponds form some of the finest wood duck habitat available. Flooded emergent vegetation that protrudes above the surface of the water provides good brood-rearing cover. Buttonbush, alder, or other shrubs that grow out of the water provide protection from aerial predators. Other emergent vegetation such as lily pads, cattails, sedges and rushes also provide insects for food in addition to places for young ducklings to hide.

You should check and maintain nest boxes during January and February of each year first by recording use from the previous summer. By examining egg membranes left over in the box, biologists and managers can estimate the number of ducks successfully hatched from each box. During maintenance checks, remove egg shells, membranes, down, and old wasp nests, and replace old nesting material such as wood shavings with new shavings. Make necessary repairs to the box and the inverted cone-shaped predator guard on the pole below the box.

Wood duck boxes as well as other types of artificial nest structures are great ways to provide habitat for wildlife. If you are interested in erecting a box on your property, proper placement and location of a wood duck box is extremely important. Placing boxes in swampy or shallow water areas with plenty of cover and emergent vegetation is important. Typical farm ponds may not be the best place for duck boxes as most have steep sides, deep edges and no emergent vegetation. Without emergent or floating vegetation, the ducklings have no place to hide and very little to eat, making them vulnerable to various predators such as snapping turtles, snakes, hawks, catfish and largemouth bass. Placing a predator guard made of aluminum flashing and shaped like an inverted cone around the pole underneath the wood duck box is just as important as the box itself. Without the guard, nest predators such as raccoons and black rat snakes will climb the pole, flush the nesting hen, slither through the entrance hole and consume the eggs.

If you have the habitat, wood ducks still need your help with nesting. For information on building wood duck nest boxes and predator guards visit the website below:

http://www.ducks.org/media/Conservation/GLARO/documents/library/landowner/WoodDuckNestBox.pdf

A BIRD, A PLANE,

OR A CRANE

I t's one of nature's most awesome spectacles, a symphony better than Bach or Beethoven that is heard from miles away free of charge every year in March and November. To the casual observer, it may first sound like a flock of Canada geese coming over very high in the sky, but it is not likely geese. I like to think that the birds are so high they may even need to be wearing oxygen masks! These months it's not likely migrating geese, as the Canada goose migration has all but disappeared from the Southeast. We do have Canada geese of course, but they are non-migratory and stay in our local area year round. It is more than likely the annual migration of the eastern population of greater sandhill cranes which cross all of Georgia and parts of Tennessee and Alabama. Their population has been constantly growing since the early 1980s. The migration of these roughly 45,000 cranes goes in full force for about a month depending on weather conditions as flock after flock of the giant, long-legged, long-necked gray birds weave their way across the Southeastern states. Their destination is their wintering grounds in south Georgia and central Florida after coming from their nesting grounds in southern Ontario, Michigan, Minnesota and Wisconsin. Apparently, Georgia is right under the direct main flight path of these handsome birds.

Occasionally, these omnivorous birds stop and rest in open agricultural fields for a few hours, to refuel temporarily with insects, worms, plant tubers, seeds, grains and mice. The birds are slate gray, stand about three feet tall and are distinguished by a bare, dark red spot behind their bill on their forehead. At maturity, they weigh 10 to12 pounds and have a wingspan of six to eight feet! In flight, their extended long neck and long legs trailing behind distinguish them from geese or herons (geese have short legs, and herons fly with their neck tucked in an "S" shaped curve against their bodies).

The most definite distinction, however, is their beautiful, almost haunting call. Their call is like a distant symphony composed of dozens of clarinets or trumpets which seems to be repeated continuously as they fly. Once heard and recognized, it is never forgotten. The mellow stereo-like sounds often emanate from several thousand feet. Sometimes the birds are barely visible from the ground and appear as specks in the sky, but their ventriloquist-like song always seems to reach the earth.

Once visually located in the sky (usually several minutes after their calls are heard), these cranes always seem to provide another curious show with their flight patterns. The flocks often seem lost or confused as some birds break off from the main flock and fly in different directions at different altitudes.

Finally, they will float back together and form a V for awhile, all heading in an organized, determined manner. This behavior is in contrast to that of geese which always seem to be more organized and stay in the "V" pattern when moving long distances. Some experts think that the cranes are spiraling vertically and appear confused because they are looking for the right wind currents and thermals to make their long flight less strenuous. Upon finding these currents, they get organized and continue on their journey. Some folks also speculate that finding the correct leader of the "V" is also the cause for some of their confusion. Who knows? The proper fearless leader seems to be real important in politics, why not in sandhill crane migration?

The best places to see and hear cranes are hilltop fields or pastures where you can escape the sounds of traffic and people in March or November. The best weather conditions are clear and sunny with a stiff tail wind. In November, that would be a prevailing northwest wind which occurs after the passage of a cold front. Of course, it would be the opposite in March.

So, the next time you're out enjoying the weather and you see or hear what appears to be a flock of Canada geese at very high altitude that make a strange haunting noise and look confused, they are probably sandhill cranes. Watch and listen for a few minutes, you'll enjoy the spectacle! The second best treat is to see the flock on the ground feeding, but you will not be able to get close to them as they prefer to land in the middle of very large fields. Sneaking up on them to get a good photo is virtually impossible because they have excellent eyesight.

ENJOYING BACKYARD WILDLIFE

The fall, winter and early spring months, depending on where you are located and what you are planting, are the ideal times to improve your backyard (or front yard) wildlife habitat. Although you can do things every month of the year to benefit wildlife that visits or inhabits your property, fall, late winter and spring are the prime times to plant trees and shrubs that will provide food and cover for numerous birds, mammals, butterflies and other critters you may enjoy watching. This is because trees and shrubs are dormant, but root growth continues later in the fall and begins breaking dormancy in early spring as soil temperatures warm. Planting in those time slots allows roots time to grow into the surrounding soil before they are stressed by heavy new top growth, drought and high summer temperatures.

Wildlife will not be the only beneficiaries of these plantings; you will enjoy the benefits also. Most landscapes today are dominated by lawns; you know, the grass you have to cut and water almost every week all summer long. Lawns are boring and monotonous and provide little value to wildlife. They demand a lot of attention from homeowners and are expensive due to fertilizer, lime, grub control, water, lawnmowers and gas. Trees, shrubs, flowerbeds, ground covers and mulched areas are much better choices for you and your wildlife. Improved habitat, greater diversity and decreased maintenance are just some of the big paybacks. Trees and shrubs add diversity to your yard and also act as wind, sound and visual barriers. They filter pollutants, provide shade, control erosion and add beauty and value to your property.

If you do have a fairly big lawn or open field, you may want to attract bluebirds to your property. They are a joy to watch and rid the local area of many undesirable insects. Build or buy a nesting box for them, put some cedar shavings in the bottom and put it on a metal pole or post about five feet above the ground facing the opening. See http://www.nabluebirdsociety.org/index.htm for bluebird nest box plans and predator guard information. If you have a big open area and want to build more than one box, place them far enough apart so that they are not within sight of each other. Some folks recommend 100 yards apart. You can put them close together (say 25 feet apart) and hope that bluebirds nest in one and swallows in the other. A male bluebird is very territorial and will not tolerate other bluebirds nesting nearby or in sight of his box.

The first step in enhancing backyard habitat is to evaluate your yard to determine moisture levels, sun and shade conditions, and soil type. By knowing this, you or a landscaper or wildlife professional can better match the tree or shrub species best suited for your region, site and growing conditions. There are so many species of beneficial native trees and shrubs that the decision can be overwhelming. Many times your search is narrowed by commercial availability and affordability.

Some of the more available native species recommended for wildlife and beautification are: flowering dogwood, various oaks, crabapples, pawpaw, wild plums, serviceberry, native hollies, persimmons, eastern red cedar, blueberries, hawthorn, elderberry, American beautyberry, red mulberry, grapes, wild pear, hazelnut and arrow wood viburnum. Some non-native (non-invasive) possibilities include butterfly bush, blazing star, and Chinese chestnut. All of these plantings will benefit dozens of wildlife species including songbirds, rabbits, raccoons, deer, wild turkeys and many more. Over time, additions to your landscape will provide a reliable source of fruit, nuts or seed along with concealment, protection, nesting and resting areas for wildlife on your land.

Whatever species you decide on, and whether you select bare-root, potted or balled-and-burlaped trees or shrubs, you should keep a few things in mind. Choose only healthy looking stock, do not allow the seedling roots to dry out, and plant them as soon as possible after you buy them. In addition, proper installation involves more than just digging a hole and setting a plant in it. If you are planting several trees or shrubs in a bed, you should incorporate about 3 inches of organic material into the top 12 inches of soil prior to planting. If you are digging individual holes, you should dig them at least two times as wide as the root ball or container, but no deeper than the container or previous planted depth. Planting too deep can result in numerous problems that usually end in poor survival. The basic idea is to thoroughly loosen the soil around the planting so the roots can easily grow. You may add lime at the time of planting, but not fertilizer, it can burn the roots.

After back-filling the hole, a thorough watering and a layer of mulch will give your planting a good start. I prefer shredded cypress mulch applied at a depth of about 2 or 3 inches out to 3 feet total diameter for most seedling trees. The first couple of years you should make sure the tree or shrub is properly watered and competing vegetation is controlled through mowing, mulching or herbicide. An annual spring application of slow-release fertilizer (many come in convenient tablet or spike form) will give your planting the nutrients they need to develop. Fertilizer application time and rates vary greatly with the plant species. You may also find it necessary to fence, stake or use a tree shelter in the early stages to protect the young seedlings from deer or rabbit browsing.

So if your habitat is lacking and you are getting cabin fever this fall or early spring, step outside, dust off your garden tools and plant some trees and shrubs in your yard. Trees and shrubs are available at nurseries, garden centers, or by catalog or internet order. For more information on creating backyard wildlife habitat or detail on location, selecting or planting vegetation for wildlife and beautification contact a wildlife biologist with your state wildlife agency. You may also find helpful information from the state forestry offices, University Cooperative Extension Service, local nurseries and garden centers.

For a more complete list of wildlife plants and more in depth planting information go to: http://pubs.cas.psu.edu/freepubs/pdfs/uh128.pdf. You can order seedlings from the National Wild Turkey Federation at http://www.outdoordealhound.com/c-174-trees.aspx. Click on trees. You can get a wealth of information on backyard wildlife and valuable wildlife plantings from the National Wildlife Federation (www.nwf.org). Finally, the internet has a wealth of backyard wildlife plantings, but be careful, as there is also some bogus information out there. Always consider the sources of planting information on trees. State and Federal agencies are almost always the best and most accurate sources of information.

So, do something about that boring yard even if it is a front yard! Plant something for wildlife, build or buy bluebird nesting boxes and dust off those binoculars to see what you are attracting or feeding. Get the kids interested too!

One of many creative backyard wildlife projects is a hummingbird and butterfly garden. It requires full sunlight, and is pretty easy to establish. There are many flower mixtures on the market including the one below.

Pennington Hummingbird & Butterfly
Garden Wildflower Seed Mixture

- 32 Ounce Bag (2 lbs) with a premium assortment of bright & cheerful annual & perennial wildflowers. See list of wild-flowers below.
- Plant in sunny to partially shaded areas.
- Most successful if planted in the spring or late fall.
- Wildflowers are a great way to enhance the beauty of your landscape. This seed mix has been selected and formulated to provide beautiful, long lasting color.

3 Steps to planting beautiful wildflowers:

1. Prepare the soil: Loosen top 2 to 3 inches of soil; Rake smooth and remove debris to create an optimal seeding area.
2. Plant the seed: evenly apply with a hand-held spreader or by hand; Rake lightly, working seed into soil 1/8-inch to 1/4-inch deep.

3. Water & fertilize seeded areas: keep soil moist until seeds have germinated; apply a seed starter fertilizer to increase seeding success.

Flower Seeds Included:

- Pheasant's Eye
- Sweet Alyssum
- Pot Marigold
- Corn Flower or Bachelor's Buttons
- Wallflower
- Shasta Daisy
- Dwarf Morning Glory
- Lance-Leaf Coreopsis
- Caliopsis or Tick Seed
- Sensation Cosmos
- Sulphur Cosmos
- Annual Forget Me Not
- Larkspur
- Dragon Flower
- California Poppy
- Blanket Flower
- Gilla
- Annual Baby's Breath
- Candytuft
- Lavatera or Mallow
- Baby Snapdragon
- Scarlet Flex
- Lupine Pixie Delight
- Perennial Lupine
- Texas Bluebonnet
- Malope
- Evening Primrose
- Shirley or Flanders Poppy
- Prairie Coneflower
- Clasping Coneflower
- Black-eyed Susan
- Annual Soapwort
- Silene

TIME FOR BIRD FEEDING

With the leaves floating to the ground in autumn, it is time for coming up with a good system for feeding our feathered friends. If you have not tried it already, you are in for a real treat and–best of all–it really helps the birds through a stressful winter season not just in the far north but even in Georgia and further south. Over 65 million Americans have participated in bird feeding and bird watching, which makes it one of the fastest growing hobbies in the country, second only to gardening. These folks also spend more than 2 billion dollars on birdseed and over 600 million on bird baths, feeders and houses every year. If you are not yet one of them, join the crowd now!

Believe it or not, there are good and not-so-good ways to feed birds, but it is pretty easy to get started. Throwing seed on the ground is not the best way to feed birds as soil contact makes the seed mold and rot as well as increases potential for disease transmission from droppings, especially bacteria such as salmonella. Feeders are a much better choice and can be homemade, purchased online or at many different local stores. Feeders can be hung or perched on a pole, post or table. This leads up to the subject of squirrels, which can be a big problem. They not only consume lots of seed, but they repel the birds and can actually ruin the feeders by chewing on them. One winter day a couple of years ago, I had 14 squirrels under my feeders in my front yard! There may not be a reasonably priced, 100 percent squirrel-proof feeder but you can get close to this by careful placement.

Do not hang feeders from tree limbs or within 10 feet of an overhanging tree limb. Easiest and best placement is on a metal pole 5 feet or more tall with a plastic or metal baffle or inverted cone about 3 feet up the pole. It looks like an upside down bowl or large dinner plate with a pole through the middle that stops the squirrel from climbing upward. I have a threaded galvanized pipe driven into the ground with a "T" on top with two three-foot horizontal pipes screwed into the "T", forming wings about six feet above the ground and parallel to it. One or two feeders can be hung from each wing depending on how many birds are attracted and what type of seed you use. This is not totally foolproof for squirrels, but it is very close. I have occasionally had a squirrel jump from the side and cling to the pole above the baffle. This can be cured by raising the baffle and spraying cooking oil on the pole.

The next important consideration is seed selection. Start with pure black oil sunflower seed, which can attract goldfinches, chickadees, woodpeckers, nuthatches and titmice. Use tube feeders encased by wire mesh to exclude squirrels and very large birds. A house-type feeder with a tray can attract cardinals, jays, purple finches, white-throated and white- crowned sparrows. A tray or platform feeder with white proso millet can attract doves, sparrows, towhees, blackbirds and cowbirds. A niger (thistle) seed feeder can attract gold and purple finches, sparrows, juncos and more. Finally, peanut butter suet can attract several species of woodpeckers, juncos, thrushes, wrens, goldfinches, cardinals and even bluebirds. The most effective way to attract the most species of birds to your yard is to put out separate feeders for each food.

Commercial seed mixes most often contain a lot of filler seeds such as cracked corn, red millet, milo, oats, wheat, rape, flax or buckwheat that are lower preference foods for our most popular backyard bird species. These will be wasted or will attract rodents and mostly undesirable birds like pigeons, starlings, blackbirds and cowbirds. Dried whole kernel corn, however, is a favorite of quail, turkeys, doves, jays and pigeons.

By the way, it is a good idea to stop feeding seed–especially sunflower seed–in early spring shortly after spring green up. There is no need to feed wild birds in spring, summer and early fall when native foods are abundant. If there are bears in the area, you definitely need to shut feeders down or the bears will visit and destroy them sooner or later. Have you ever seen a wooden or plastic feeder that bears have visited? It is not a pretty sight!

Finally, buy a hummingbird feeder and keep it full of sugar water (four parts water to one part white granulated sugar) from early spring through summer and into late fall. This will help fuel hummer migrants moving north or south in addition to the summer native ruby throats nesting near your yard through spring and summer. Once the hatchlings fly out of their nest, they will join the crowd at the feeder making life more interesting as they zoom around chasing each other away from the feeder. The consensus seems to be that they are fighting in an effort to defend their territory, which includes the feeder.

Males and females are both quite territorial and defend about one quarter of an acre, which includes their nest and the feeder. One way to reduce fighting is to put up two or more feeders in close proximity so aggressive birds cannot defend all of the feeders.

For more information on feeding birds and seed, go to: www.gohuntgeorgia.com/documentdetail.aspx?docid=142&pageid=1&cat egory=conservation

This site also contains helpful links to other important bird feeding sites. No matter where you live, it is time to get started feeding birds, both nesters and spring and fall migrants, especially when native food sources are low or scarce. Go for it, you will not regret it!

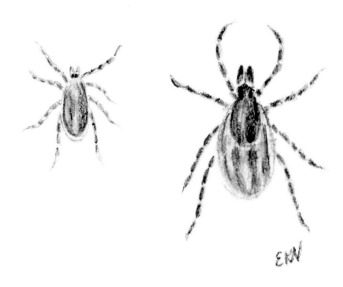

LYME DISEASE:

DANGERS, PREVENTION &
TREATMENT

m I a tick expert? No, but I have been through the mill when it comes to ticks and tick-borne diseases. Several years ago, I found a tick crawling on my shirt after a short tour of my front yard recently. Soon after that, I picked four, big, blood-engorged ticks off my yellow lab who lives mostly in our front yard. Is this a little too close for comfort? Yes! I am a little gun shy about ticks, and you will see why later in this chapter. This bad tick news may give us a clue as to how many ticks are active in the woods in spring, summer and fall. Even the mountains, where ticks used to be rare, seem to have an increasing population. The tick situation has been more worrisome in the Southeast since the proven occurrence of Lyme disease. Add it to the worrisome list of tick-borne diseases already here which includes Rocky Mountain Spotted Fever, Ehrlichiosis, Babesiosis, Anaplasmosis, Southern Tick Associated Rash Illness (STARI) and who knows what else. These bacterial diseases can be transmitted by the bite of a tick once the tick is attached to you or your pets for 24 hours or more.

Why is this important to outdoor enthusiasts? It can't happen to you, right? Wrong! It happened to me twice. The first time was shortly after the turn of the century. I pulled a tick off my lower body about two days after returning from a turkey hunt in Wilkes County, near Athens, Georgia. It itched, but that was the only symptom. One day later the ball game changed when I developed a sudden high fever (103+) and felt achy and weak all over. I called my doctor and went in to see him the same day. My doc has been around for awhile, not just street-wise but also woods-wise, and I had been his patient for over 20 years. I told him about removing the tick, and he did not even flinch while writing a prescription for the common antibiotic Doxycycline to start that same day. He said we would get a blood sample to send it to the lab to test for Lyme disease but there was no sense waiting for results to start treatment as Doxycycline will cure most tick-borne diseases including Lyme (see Table 1 at the end of this chapter).

Within 24 hours my fever had subsided, and within 48, I was feeling almost as good as new but kept taking the drug as instructed for the entire 10-day round. Meanwhile the blood test came back inconclusive (as was very common back in those days) but doc and I are fully convinced that I had contracted Rocky Mountain Spotted Fever and we had caught it so early that the spots had not even had time to develop (see Table 1).

Fast forward to May 2005. I had just returned from a successful turkey hunt in New Hampshire, and my belly was itching and showing some redness. New Hampshire is a hot spot for Lyme disease. (Note how turkey hunting seems to get me in trouble a lot).

I didn't think much about it for a week or so. Then I got a flashlight and discovered a tick embedded on my navel! I could not believe it. My wife carefully plucked it off and we put some alcohol on the site.

Well, things progressively got worse. The bite was still somewhat red and itchy, but there was no huge red area and no bulls-eye (see Table 1). I ran a low grade fever (99-100) two or three times a week. Stiffness was developing in my hands, neck and shoulders and progressively getting worse until I could not close my hands to make a fist when first awakening in the morning (with sore neck and shoulders, too). It took 10 to 15 minutes of flexing and running hot water over my hands to regain normal movement.

My wife put two and two together first, connecting the tick bite and my symptoms. She finally convinced me to go to the doctor in mid-July. It was Doxycycline and blood tests once again.

Symptoms improved in a few days and the fever went away. Blood tests came back apparently inconclusive but somewhat suspicious. Two weeks after completing the round of antibiotics, all my symptoms came back.

Another longer round of antibiotics was prescribed and completed with temporarily good results. But no cigar, the symptoms returned again! My doc referred me to an infectious diseases specialist. Within 10 minutes she told me intravenous (IV) antibiotics was the next step, every day for a month. I tried to talk her out of it, but it did not work. After several failed attempts with big needles, an 18-inch PIC-line was finally inserted in my vein near my right elbow. It ran all the way to within an inch from the top of my heart. You have to understand how much I hate needles!

Home health nurses helped me get started and changed my dressings every three days. It took me an hour every day to hook up to the antibiotic bag, drip the solution in through the line, finish up with a syringe full of heparin (to keep the line from clotting) and disconnect everything. But after a month it was still not working!

She wanted me to go for one more week. I did, and it still was not working. She removed the 18-inch long PIC-line, pulled it out like she was removing a snake, and referred me to a rheumatologist. Is this a horror story yet?

With a referral from a prominent doctor friend, a highly renowned rheumatologist in Gainesville agreed to see me quickly. She ran some more blood tests, asked a lot of questions and put me on steroids and an arthritis drug called Methotrexate. After careful examination of two previous Lyme test results (including fine-print footnotes) along with her tests, she concluded that I did not have Lyme disease and also did not have rheumatoid arthritis. Her diagnosis was auto-immune arthritis, which is characterized by the body attacking its own immune system. So, I did not get this from the tick, right? She explained that it could have easily come from the tick as there is still much to learn and many undiscovered tick-borne diseases.

Before this rheumatologist came to Gainesville, she had practiced for years in Connecticut (the ground zero of Lyme disease) and treated thousands of Lyme patients. I don't doubt she knows more about Lyme treatment than anyone in Georgia. I wish I had found her first before going to the infectious disease specialist!

Finally, in July 2006, I went in to the doctor's office for a seven-hour drip infusion of a new arthritis drug called Rituxan. Two weeks later, a follow up infusion was administered for four hours. Although this drug has worked wonders for many recipients, it did not seem to cause much improvement in my case.

Fast forward again to evaluate my condition in the spring of 2012. My fever is gone but other symptoms are still there at a reduced and tolerable level, especially my stiff hands. I'm still taking Methotrexate every week and getting blood work done on liver function and other parameters every three to four months.

According to the American Lyme Disease Foundation: "Worldwide, there are about 850 tick species and 30 major tick-borne diseases; the U.S. alone has 82 species of ticks collectively causing 10 major diseases. New tick-borne diseases continue to be discovered. For example, Anaplasmosis was first described in 1994; a Lyme disease-like illness has recently been reported in Missouri that does not test positive on standard Lyme disease tests and is thought to be transmitted by the Lone Star tick; and an encephalitis-like virus was discovered in 1997 in several deer ticks in New England. Some researchers suspect that there are even more tick-borne diseases that are still unidentified."

Lyme disease is much more common in the Northeastern states than it is in the Southeast (see Table 1). Preliminary studies indicate an infection rate in ticks of less than one percent in most areas of Georgia. However, Rocky Mountain Spotted Fever and Erlichiosis are common in this state, especially south of a line from Athens to Columbus. This is mainly due to higher tick populations south of this line. How can we avoid, prevent, or treat Lyme disease and all the other tick-borne diseases? First of all, prevention is the best cure. From April through September, the woods will have the highest active tick populations of the year. Ticks lie in wait for passing hosts by sitting on tall grass, leaves and vegetation. When they feel body heat, they drop off onto a passing host. Most ticks enter our bodies through pants cuffs, at the beltline and at the neck.

Before entering the woods this time of year, plan to wear knee-high boots with high socks and tuck your pants legs into the socks. Seal the junction with masking tape. Tuck your shirt into your pants, and wear a tight belt. Wear light colored clothing so that crawling ticks can be readily seen and picked off before they attach. Insect repellents are often quite effective. The best of these for ticks are products called Permanone or Duranon. Both contain 0.5 percent Permethrin. They must be sprayed on clothing (not on skin) and both are effective repellents for ticks, chiggers, mosquitoes and other insects. Generally, the common insect repellents sprayed on the skin and containing DEET are largely ineffective in repelling ticks.

Upon returning from your woodland excursion, check your body carefully for attached ticks and remove them promptly, but carefully, with a pair of pointed tweezers. First, swab the site with rubbing alcohol. Grasp the tick by the head as close to the attachment point as possible. Do not grasp it by the body! Gently pull the tick directly upward off your body and treat the bite with alcohol. Do not use petroleum jelly, a hot match, dishwashing liquid or any other irritant in an attempt to get the tick to back out.

Ticks that were attached should be saved in a jar of alcohol in case any rash or other symptoms of Lyme disease develop. This is one big mistake that I made in both of my tick episodes. Identifying the tick species is one key to diagnosing the disease. Watch the bite carefully for any signs of the disease. The most common early sign is a slowly expanding red rash which may fade in the center as it moves away from the tick bite. However, only 60 to 80 percent of infected individuals will develop the rash. Other symptoms include mild headaches, swollen lymph nodes, stiff and painful muscles and joints, fatigue, and low fever (in the case of RMSF it is most often high fever, and this is the first symptom to develop).

Symptoms may occur several days to weeks after a tick bite. Consult your physician immediately if you suspect that you may have Lyme disease. In its early stages, it is now easily detected by a single blood test and easily treated by antibiotics such as Doxycycline. This is not always the case with other tick-borne diseases as I found out the hard way. Later stages can be more difficult to cure and can have serious symptoms such as chronic arthritis, irregular heartbeat, dizziness, headache, stiff neck, facial palsy, meningitis, and weakness.

Tick-borne diseases are a serious matter, they are not a cause for panic! Your chances of getting diseases from a tick are pretty slim, especially if you exercise some simple precautions (as explained on the adjacent page) and are aware of the common symptoms of the disease and monitor for these carefully. A wealth of information is available at www.aldf.com/ the website of American Lyme Disease Foundation. It is an excellent, informative website that will answer all your questions on all of the tick-borne diseases. See deer tick pictures from ALDF below.

Finally, don't avoid the woods just because of ticks. You will be missing out on lots of outdoor fun! As the police captain on Hill Street Blues used to say to his officers every morning, "Be careful out there."

The Deer tick (*Ixodes scapularis*)

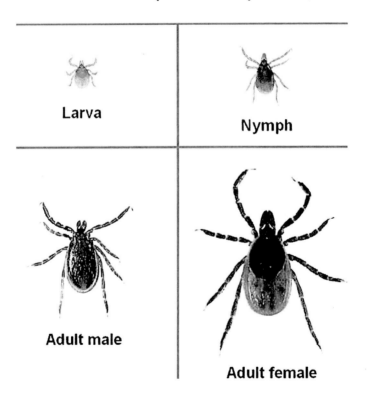

Larva

Nymph

Adult male

Adult female

Table 1. Tick-Borne Diseases Comparison Chart

	Tick Vector	Bacterium	Prevalence Area	Early Symptoms	Long Term	Treatment
Lyme Disease	deer tick aka black legged tick	spirochete	Northeast, Upper Midwest	expanding rash 3-30 days after bite, joint pain, fever	stiff neck, tingling numbness, arthritis	Doxycycline
Rocky Mtn. Spotted Fever (RMSF)	American dog tick, Brown dog tick, lone star tick	rickettsia	Southeast	fever in 2-14 days, rash, nausea, vomiting, severe headache, muscle pain	abdominal pain, joint pain, diarrhea	Doxycycline
Ehrlichiosis (HME)	lone star tick	rickettsia	South of line & W. Texas	Occur within 1 week fever, headaches, malaise, muscle pain, chills	Not common	Doxycycline
Anaplasmosis (HGE)	deer tick aka black-legged tick	rickettsia	Northeast, S. New Jersey Upper Midwest	Occur within 1 week fever, headaches, malaise, muscle pain, chills	Not common	Doxycycline
Babesiosis	deer tick aka black-legged tick	protozoan	Northeast, Upper Midwest	malaise, anorexia, fatigue, fever, sweats, muscle pain	symptoms may abate then re-occur	oral quinine + clindamcin
Southern Tick Associated Rash Illness (STARI)	lone star tick	spirochete	S. of line New Jersey to Texas	similar to Lyme, lesions smaller, fatigue	Not common	Doxycycline

This chart adapted from American Lyme Disease Foundation

THE BOSS, A TRUE MENTOR

One day, years ago, the Boss was hunting elk, as he often did on his north woods hunting club in New Hampshire. Deer and wild hog hunting seasons were also open, but they were always secondary to elk.

He had tracked a small herd of elk slowly up the mountain until finally, up ahead and over a knoll, he could see the neck and head of a cow elk stretching upward to feed on buds from tree limbs. She presented a long shot, even for the Boss, and there was no rest, but he aimed for the neck and squeezed the trigger. The gun fired and the Boss looked up, but there had been no apparent reaction from the cow elk. Her head and long neck were still reaching for buds.

Bang! He fired a second shot, looked up and still the cow had not moved. Confused and frustrated, the Boss chambered and fired a third round into the neck of the elk, and then it disappeared. All was quiet.

"Well, it either ran off or it's dead," the Boss muttered to himself. He walked up the hill and over the knoll and found three dead elk, all shot cleanly through the neck and dropped in their tracks in an area no bigger than your living room! The antlerless elk quota that year was three. The Boss had inadvertently filled his annual quota in less than one minute!

The remainder of that hunt was spent dragging and skinning elk. They would make up the entree of a special invitation game dinner at his restaurant, the Old Riverton Inn.

Some of us called him "The Boss" because we had worked for him many years ago in his restaurant. Others called him Jim or Jimmy. I hunted with him at his very exclusive northern hunting club for 35 years. Another friend, Paul, had been making the trip for more than 45 years.

The Boss was an Italian Catholic—a stout, strong, rather short man with a Friar Tuck bald head, prominent nose, square jaw and a permanent twinkle in his pale blue eyes. His hunting attire was the traditional red and black plaid wool jacket and pants with a matching wool cap. He carried a .30-06 Manlicher-Sauer bolt-action rifle with a 4X Leupold scope that he bought sometime in the late 1950s.

If there was ever a true friend and hunting buddy, it was the Boss. He was a gentleman, a sportsman, a kind and generous man who grew up the hard way and worked hard his whole life. He also worked hard at hunting and fishing, taking great pains to make sure his guests were entertained, well-fed and accommodated.

He survived the Great Depression and told us many times that his staple diet in those days was boiled wild milkweed and fresh woodchuck—when his family had enough money to buy him the bullets to shoot one.

His origins from a poor family in a utilitarian generation shaped his life as a hunter and fisherman who enjoyed the chase but still meant to bring home the bacon. For many years, he and his wife, Mildred, hosted an annual game dinner at his restaurant that was attended by a hundred people or more who shared in his harvest of elk, deer, wild hog and other game. His signature dish as the chef at his own restaurant was elk burgundy, which always drew raves from the guests.

I first hunted with the Boss in 1966, when I was a junior in high school. I got lucky and shot a wild hog only 30 minutes into my first hunt and was hooked for life. I never got a chance to do these things with my dad, who did not hunt or fish, so the Boss was filling a void for me. In the early years, my role was clear—to help him get meat for the annual game dinner. For the most part, with some patient instruction from the Boss, I did pretty well in that role, dragging hogs, deer and an occasional elk out of the woods on a regular basis.

At the hunt camp in the evening, we would swap stories and take turns telling what we had seen during the day. The Boss then instructed us on how to stalk hunt very slowly through the woods, taking only one or two steps at a time then stopping for a minute or more, so we could glimpse the game before they spotted us.

The Boss's ultimate trophy was not a 6x6 bull elk, but rather a 200 to 250-lb pound calf elk, which served as the top item on his menu for the game dinner. Calf elk steaks were the ultimate in fine cuisine. Cow elk would substitute fairly well, but bull elk were scorned because, as the Boss said, "You couldn't cut the gravy with a knife." The Boss had taken his share of trophy bull elk in the early years, but had enough of the dragging and quartering and back breaking work that went into getting a bull out of the woods for the return of a marginal piece of meat. He had no use for the antlers. The connection between hunting and meat was crystal clear to him.

In our constant quest for the calf elk, there were several stories that the Boss told and retold at the hunt camp every year with amazing detail and accuracy, just as if it happened yesterday. He was not one to exaggerate or embellish—he did not have to, his stories were just right the way they were. It was like a home-coming every year in camp as freshly retold stories became just as exciting as the first time they were told, even though we knew every word.

The Boss was an honest man without a trace of ego, which caused him to forego the stories of the great trophy hunt or the great kill in favor of human nature stories or strange and amusing events. He told short stories, like the one about his old deceased friend and hunting partner, Andy, Paul's dad, who was hunting one morning in fresh, deep snow when he stepped up on top of a snow-covered rock. He couldn't understand why he felt a little dizzy, even queasy, until he figured out that the rock was moving! Only when a big wild hog scooted out from under his feet and dumped him on his back did he realize what was going on!

Other of the Boss's stories were longer, but just as welcome and entertaining. He loved to talk about Carmine, a feisty little Italian guy with a big heart and a slightly off-kilter perspective on the world. Carmine was the Boss's butcher and best friend. He had no sense of direction and did not believe in maps or compasses. On more than one occasion he got lost within 100 yards of the road. As darkness fell, he would begin to panic and would shoot up all of his ammunition in volleys of three so that the Boss could locate him and call him out to the road—he was always lost within shouting distance of a road.

Carmine woke up at the crack of dawn one day to find a nice buck feeding under an apple tree across the field from the cabin. Still in his long johns, he cracked open the front door, crawled on his belly across the porch and braced for a prone shot. Bang! At the same moment that the buck bounded off, sleeping hunters popped straight up, bumping their heads on bunk beds, and a large chunk of wood splintered off the end of the brand new cabin porch and went airborne. Carmine didn't see the end of the porch through his scope, but his rifle barrel had it dead-centered! The club superintendent was heard the next week cussing the crazy person who had "Stuck an ax in the end of his brand new porch."

Then there were the meat stories. In camp one icy cold December, we had to rent a trailer to haul our bountiful three-day harvest of a cow elk and two nice deer. The trailer was full of carcasses, camp was cleaned, and everyone except Carmine was ready to go home. As daylight turned to dusk, we heard several loud bangs as shot after shot rang out from Carmine's gun. He must have fired 12 or 14 shots. We all winced and imagined dead boar and deer lying everywhere and thought about how long it would take us to field dress and drag out all that game. Worse, we had no space left in the trailer! The Boss took it all in stride, Harry the surgeon paced nervously, Paul was calculating the options of renting another trailer or a bigger one, and I was sharpening my knife, getting ready to do some field dressing. Finally, emerging from the darkness with a sheepish grin, Carmine confessed to missing upwards of 6 or 8 hogs and deer as they paraded down the same snowy trail one by one and jumped over a log just like they do in a shooting gallery. He said his gun probably needed sighting in. We laughed until we cried—mostly from relief.

Carmine was famous for his poor shooting. Invariably, he would see more game than anyone else, but he seemed to have problems putting game on the ground. Rather than find fault with himself, he was constantly blaming his gun. "This scope is off, Jim. It needs sighting in," was a constant complaint from Carmine. The Boss would set targets up, and Carmine would take careful aim. Part of the problem was that he never seemed to get a steady rest, even against a car hood, cabin post or tree. Bang! "This damn thing is shooting 3 inches high and to the left," he would say. "I'm changing the scope." Click-click-click.

He would then take careful aim again, but the Boss, standing behind Carmine, could plainly see that his gun-barrel never stopped moving. Weaving, bobbing, wobbling, rocking and then Bang! "This thing is still off!" Click-click-click. No amount of pleading from the Boss would convince Carmine that his scope was not off and that his aim was unsteady. No matter where his scope was really set, his fate was sealed and he was destined to be off even with a "good rest." No one, least of all Carmine, ever knew where his gun was really shooting.

At the opposite end of the hunting spectrum in our camp was Harry, a skilled surgeon who ran on precision, accuracy and pure ego. He was an excellent shot and never let anyone forget it. Every trip was blessed with stories of how some deer or hog dropped like a ton of bricks, shot in the neck by his Weatherby .257 Roberts at 200 yards or better. His ammo cost about $2.50 a round, so he couldn't afford to waste a shot. At least that's what he told us.

Hunt camp was a particularly great place to be when the Boss got his own calf elk. We were hunting one evening when I heard a shot nearby. I knew that it had to be the Boss, so I trudged through the snow toward the shot. In a little while, I saw him, walking slowly and staring at the snow. He said he thought he had made a good shot but the calf elk had run off. There were tracks in the snow, but no blood. Then we found a little blood, just a few drops, but it was getting dark. The Boss didn't want to quit even though the 300-yard blood trail quickly became more like a half mile. Eventually, he pointed and said, "Shoot him!" As the wounded animal got up and lunged forward in an effort to get away, I put a bullet in its neck. The Boss said, "Great job!" just like I had done all the work.

By the time we had field-dressed the elk, it was pitch dark and we had no flashlight. I was worried and had no idea which way to walk, never mind drag that elk. The Boss said, "Don't worry. This elk made almost a complete circle after it was wounded. We're not far from where I shot it. The truck is that way." I didn't believe him, but I didn't want to say anything, either. He insisted on dragging the kill, even though he was close to 70 years old at the time. Side by side, we pulled 20 or 30 yards at a time, then rested. Even a calf elk weighs 225 or 250 pounds, field dressed— and that's dead weight. All we could see was snow and thousands of stars, there was no moon that night. We finally broke out into a clearing and I could barely see the truck parked on the far side of the field. I was overwhelmed with relief. The Boss knew exactly where we were the whole time.

Then there was the "Great Storm." It must have hit back in the late 1960s, if my memory serves me. Paul, Carmine and the Boss, went to bed at a remote cabin one balmy November night with a thunderstorm brewing in the distance. They woke up the next morning with three feet of fresh snow on the ground! All thoughts of hunting vanished and were replaced with concern about how they were going to get out of there. They were driving an old Scout—a tough 4X4, but no match for three feet of snow. By pushing snow ahead of the bumper until they stopped, then backing up and ramming the snow again, they were able to get a couple of hundred feet away from the cabin and toward the gate. Finally, the road was totally obliterated as the uneven ground got more uneven by mounting snow depth, and the Scout laid over on its side and made its last gasp. It was time to trudge out to the gate and down to the nearest house, more than two miles away. The Boss led the way making leg holes in the deep snow for Paul and Carmine to step into. By nightfall, they made it out and phoned for help. The next day, a truck with chains, a plow and a winch finally got the Scout out.

The Boss did his last hunting in October 2000, on the opening weekend of elk season. Even though he couldn't get far from the truck, he had a great time. For us, it was a fitting end for the century and the beginning of a legend. Having survived two heart valve replacement surgeries, the Boss passed away in his sleep in February 2001 at the age of 87. Well before he died, though, the Boss made careful arrangements for Paul, by now a 45-year veteran of the hunt club, to take over his membership. Paul is also a kind and gracious host, but we all know it will never be the same without the Boss. Even with all my fond memories, there is emptiness in my heart that will never be filled. The Boss etched a permanent mark on my soul.

It hurts to think that I'll never hunt with him again or hear another of his stories. I would like to tell him what his friendship and woodsmanship teachings have meant to me. Perhaps I have not fully learned it yet. I've been honored to have met a lot of wonderful people in my life, but few have had the impact of the Boss. He gave me a pastime that became a career and a passion for the outdoors which will last the rest of my life. Each time I go to the woods, whether it's on the old hunting club property or somewhere near my Georgia home, I think about the Boss and those times. I know that when I put my gun away for the last time, thoughts of the Boss and the hunting camp will be close by, reminding me of why I am a hunter and of what the outdoors has given me.

Thank you, Boss.

KENT KAMMERMEYER

- Graduated with B.S. degree in wildlife management from University of Connecticut in 1972.

- Received M.S. in wildlife biology from University of Georgia (UGA) in 1975.

- Recipient of **Stoddard – Sutton Wildlife Conservation Award (1977)** for outstanding achievement as a student at UGA.

- Worked for Georgia DNR Wildlife Resources Division for 30 years, most of it as a Senior Wildlife Biologist.

- Recipient of **Wildlife Biologist of the Year Award in 1983** for outstanding achievement in wildlife management from GA DNR.

- Chairman of GA White-tailed Deer Committee for over 25 years until retirement. Three White-tailed Deer Plans developed by committee in this time period.

- As chairman, became senior author of three booklets **Deer Herd Management for Georgia Hunters, Feral Hogs in Georgia: Disease, Damage & Control in 2003** and **Controlling Deer Damage in Georgia in 2001.**

- Compiled, analyzed and modeled deer harvest data for **57 WMAs (7,000 deer annually)** in Georgia. Project ongoing for 27 years.

- Directly supervised 8 Wildlife Technicians and 6 WMAs totaling 150,000 acres in Northeastern GA.

- Published over **50 scientific papers and over 350 popular articles** mostly on deer.

- Since 1999, published over **70 Plant Species Profiles** columns for Quality Whitetails magazine, two per issue in every issue.

- Developed two chapters (**Baiting** and **Supplemental Feeding**) for REPORT ON DEER MANAGEMENT ISSUES FOR THE SOUTHEAST by The Wildlife Society Deer Committee (2001).

- Received the Southeastern Director's award "**Wildlife Biologist of the Year**" for the year 2000. First ever GA recipient.

- Received the "**Best Game Paper**" award from the Southeastern Section of The Wildlife Society at the **1975** and the **2000** Southeastern Association of Fish & Wildlife Agencies Conferences.

- Received the **2005 Deer Management Career Achievement Award** for Outstanding Contributions to White-tailed Deer Management in the Southeastern United States from The Deer Committee of the

Southeastern Section of the Wildlife Society. First state biologist ever to receive this award.

- **Senior Technical Advisor** for the Quality Deer Management Association (QDMA) from 7/05-10/06.

- Co-Editor and Co-Author for **"Quality Food Plots, Your Guide to Better Deer and Better Deer Hunting"** a 310 page full color book published by QDMA and available at www.qdma.com .

- Co-Editor and Senior Author for **"Deer & Turkey Management Beyond Food Plots"** available at www.deerconsulting.com.

- Currently doing part time wildlife consulting (with over 50 clients in the Southeast) and freelance writing mostly on deer and deer food plots.

EDITH K. VASSAR

E dee lives in Granby, Connecticut, with her husband
Michael and their flat coat retriever, Zen. Surrounded
by a wildlife refuge, her home is an idyllic spot to
study wildlife. She enjoys bird feeding (especially hummers),
bluebirds and bluebird boxes, and frequent observation of deer
and wild turkeys. She and Mike enjoy occasional observations or
visits from coyotes and black bears. See her bear sketch on the
front cover based on personal experience in her front yard! Once,
another bold bear got a refreshing drink of water from her pool
on a warm summer day but thankfully decided not to take a
swim!

Edee's natural love and appreciation for the beauty of nature
has been and is continually enhanced by her older brother Kent's
knowledge of the local flora and fauna. Drawing and painting
wildlife is a hobby and passion which she hopes to continue and
improve upon for many years to come.

She is proud to be the mother of a lovely daughter, Katy, and grandmother to delightful Avery Rose. A nurse practitioner by profession, with Master's degrees in both nursing and public health, she delivers primary health care as part of a family practice in a nearby town.